The Path of Integrity

Teachings from the Lineage of the Warrior, Scholar and Sage

By Jim Moltzan

Disclaimer

This book is intended for information purposes only. The author does not promise or imply any results to those using this information, nor are they responsible for any adverse results brought about by the usage of the information contained herein. Use the information provided at your own risk. Furthermore, the author does not guarantee that the holder of this information will improve his or her health from the information contained herein.

The author of this book has used his/her best efforts in preparing this book. The author makes no representation of warranties with respect to the accuracy, applicability, or completeness of the contents of this book.

This book is © copyrighted by CAD Graphics, Inc. No part of this may be copied, or changed in any form, sold, or used in any way other than what is outlined within this book under any circumstances. No part of this book may be reproduced or transferred in any form or by any means, graphic, electronic, or mechanical, including photocopying, recording, taping, or by any information storage retrieval system, without the written permission of the author.

© 2025 CAD Graphics, Inc.

ISBN: 978-1-958837-45-0

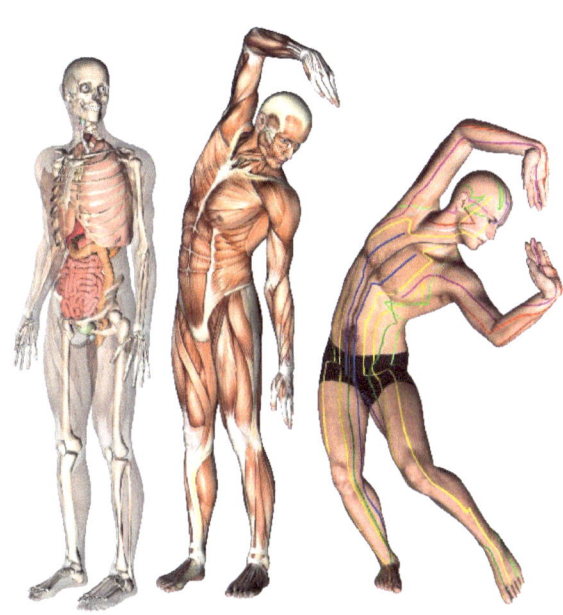

We are the architect of our own health, happiness, destiny, or fate.

Life is an echo.

What you send, comes back.

What you give, you get.

What you see in others, exists in you.

Remember, life is an echo.

It always get back to you.

So give goodness.

Table of Contents

Foreword 1
   Why I Share, What I Have Learned 2
SECTION I: THE PATH OF INTEGRITY 3
Introduction: The Eternal Path 4
Foundations of the Path 4
   1. Path of Integrity and The Way of Dissonance: Our Inner Battle 4
   2. Knowing the Self 5
   3. True Living: Learn and Earn 5
Building the Inner Temple 6
   4. Be Your Own Guard 6
   5. Teach with Wisdom 6
   6. Build with Patience 7
   7. Seek Correct Understanding 7
Walking the Way 8
   8. Avoid Seeking Attention 8
   9. Think Correctly, Avoid Foolishness 8
   10. Respond as a Person of Balance 9
The Living Legacy 9
   11. Leave Behind Good Seeds 9
   12. Seek the Face of Honor 10
   13. Change Your Reality 10
   14. Become a Living Vessel of Wisdom 11
   15. Inner Cultivation: The Inner Art of Vitality 11
   16. The Seed of Peace 12
SECTION II: ESSAYS 13
   A: Spiritual Paradoxes & Theological Reflections 14
      Spiritual Paradoxes: Humility Taught, Materialism Practiced 14
      Do We Die and Go to Heaven, or Die and Bring Heaven with Us? 17
      If Jesus Returned Today 19
      Drinking from the Well, Denying the Source 23
      The Upside-Down King: A Lesson in Humility, Wisdom, and True Power 26

B: Eastern Philosophy, Metaphysics & Inner Alchemy 28
- From Wuji to Tai Chi 28
- The Threefold Way: Society, Nature, and Self in Chinese Philosophy 32
- The Buddhist Eightfold Path & the Taoist 8 Keys of Wisdom 34
- Wind and Water, Makes Fire 39
- Gong De Wei Shen 42
- The Warrior, the Scholar, and the Sage 46
- "Man Divides Heaven and Earth" 52
- "Heaven and Earth, Turned Upside Down" 54
- "Born With Nothing, Die With Nothing" 56

C: Moral Psychology, Truth & Perception 58
- Philosophy or Religion? 58
- True, Right, and Correct 64
- Beyond Critical Thinking: The True, Right, and Correct Framework 65
- "They Don't Know, What They Don't Know" – The Dunning-Kruger Effect 69
- Become the Diamond, Leave the Coal Behind 72
- Mastery in the World of Form: Integrating Wealth, Health, and Spirit 74
- The Eight Keys of Wisdom 77

D: Emotional Intelligence & Healing from Trauma 80
- Seek Out the "Wounded Healers" 80
- Unseen Wounds: How Emotional Trauma Shapes Our Health 83
- The Misogi Challenge 87
- Uri, Jeong, Qing, and Camaraderie: A Cross-Cultural Study of Emotional Bonds 93

E: Cultural Commentary & Social Reflections 97
- Wealth Without Wellness is Poverty in Disguise 97
- Do Recreational Sports and Religions Exist in Separate Domains? 100
- Rough Initiations – Rites of Passage 104
- Ancient Paths, Modern Peace: The Many Names of Enlightenment 109

PART III: MYSTICISM & INTERNAL TRADITIONS 112
- Understanding the Korean Lunisolar Calendar and Mystical Time Cycles 113
- Korean Neigong: Internal Cultivation Systems 119
- Exploring Wei Dan, Qigong, and Nei Dan 130

   Exploring the Thin Line Between Martial Legend and Human Potential 135

   Feasibility and Legacy of Extensive Martial Arts Systems in the Modern Age 141

   Chamsa Meditation 159

   Degrees of Control: Psychological Lessons from a Closed Community 165

SECTION IV: APPENDICES 177

   Sources & Influences 177

   Glossary 180

   About the Instructor, Author & Artist - Jim Moltzan 184

   Books Available Through Amazon 186

   Other Products 188

CONTACTS 189

Foreword

This book marks both a continuation and a turning point in my life's work.

In **Warrior, Scholar, Sage,** I sought to synthesize decades of physical training, internal cultivation, and philosophical inquiry into a unified system of personal development. That work was grounded in the archetypes that shaped me: the disciplined warrior, the seeking scholar, and the reflective sage. It served as a compass and a map for those ready to undertake the path of strength, knowledge, and wisdom. But *The Path of Integrity* goes deeper.

It is not simply a refinement of earlier teachings. It is the voice that emerged after walking through fire. It is the fruit of long nights of unlearning, of listening inwardly, and of standing still long enough to see the root system beneath everything I once thought I understood.

This book carries the lessons not only of discipline, but of paradox. Not only of mastery, but of humility. Not only of training, but of transformation. It addresses wounds, seen and unseen, and the healing that occurs when we stop pretending we are unbreakable.

Where my earlier books taught structure, systems, and embodied tradition, this book speaks more intimately. It is equal parts essay, reflection, journal, and transmission. It blends wisdom from ancient paths with insights gathered through spiritual inquiry, trauma recovery, and cross-cultural observation. It is for those who are no longer satisfied with performing wellness, but who are ready to live aligned with truth. Even when it's inconvenient.

If *Warrior, Scholar, Sage* was about learning how to walk with purpose, The Path of Integrity is about learning how to stand still with courage. It is about listening to the silent voice of principle when the world shouts confusion. It is about discerning the way forward when maps no longer help.

I offer these words not as conclusions, but as invitations. Each page a doorway, each essay a mirror. This book is not a rulebook. It is a companion for those who refuse to settle for shallow living. It is for those who sense there is a deeper current, and who are ready to return to it.

Welcome to the Path.

—Jim Moltzan

Why I Share, What I Have Learned

I made my commitment many years ago to learn, study, practice and teach fitness and well-being. My education came from martial arts and various other Eastern methods rooted in Traditional Chinese Medicine (TCM). I started when I was 16 years old and have never stopped since; 61 now.

I have written journals, produced educational graphics and co-authored a book in addition to many that I have self-authored. I blog often with a WordPress site, writing about the anatomical, physiological and mental benefits of mind and body training. Years back I started recording my classes and lectures, knowing that somewhere down the line, all of this information would be valuable to those who need and desire it.

My YouTube channel has almost 300 videos of FREE classes and other education videos. The goal all along has been to raise the awareness that Tai chi (a martial art), qigong (yoga at its root) and many other Eastern wellness methods, have proven the test of time for maintaining well-being. No gym, no mat, no membership, no special clothes or equipment. Just the individual and their engagement.

Weak or injured knees, back issues (strains & sciatica), stress & anxiety, asthma, arthritis, balance, poor posture - the list is endless. These are all issues that can be improved or overcome by those serious about learning about the mind, body & spirit connection.

SECTION I: THE PATH OF INTEGRITY

Introduction: The Eternal Path

Life is not a random sequence of moments, but a sacred opportunity. A test of our awareness, discipline, and choices. From the breath of our birth to the silence of our final exhale, we are continually asked to remember where we came from, how we are to live, and what we will leave behind. The Path of Integrity is not merely a code of conduct but a sacred alignment with principles that guide us toward harmony, insight, and service. It is a path illuminated by clarity, sustained by inner strength, and tested daily.

In contrast, the Way of Dissonance is the path of confusion, distraction, and selfishness. It lures us with ease and gratification but leaves us hollow and imbalanced. Whereas Integrity brings us into alignment with the deeper flow of life, Dissonance severs that connection, dividing us from others and from our own deeper nature.

Across cultures and belief systems, a shared understanding emerges: our earthly life is temporary, and its purpose is spiritual growth. At the end of our life, many traditions hold that we must face a divine judgment. Not of material accomplishments but of character, impact, and the seeds we have sown in others. Whether or not one adheres to a particular religion, this principle of sowing and reaping, cause and effect, holds true.

The visible world is fleeting. The invisible exists in the character, peace, wisdom, and honor we cultivate, endures. Like a single day, life offers morning (birth and innocence), noon (activity and responsibility), and night (reflection and transition). Each part must be lived with sacred intention.

Foundations of the Path

1. Path of Integrity and The Way of Dissonance: Our Inner Battle

Each moment offers a choice. One path is the *Path of Integrity* which leads toward spiritual awakening, inner peace, and meaningful legacy. The other, the *Way of Dissonance*, feeds illusion, distracts the mind, and blinds us to our deeper purpose.

Integrity demands discipline, service, humility, and spiritual courage. It asks us to see beyond ourselves and to live for what uplifts others and brings order to our relationships, thoughts, and actions.

Dissonance, on the other hand, tempts us to follow our impulses, indulge resentment, or chase fleeting pleasures. Its cost is disconnection from our deeper self, from nature, from community, and from the divine.

To walk with Integrity is to become a guardian of our mind, a caretaker of our energy, and a steward of truth. To follow Dissonance is to drift, reacting to life rather than shaping it consciously. As taught by many sages: *"Stillness is the voice of destiny."* When we are quiet and inwardly alert, we can perceive our next correct step.

2. Knowing the Self

The first step on the Warrior-Scholar-Sage path is self-knowing. Without knowing who we truly are in our values, nature, strengths, weaknesses, we cannot walk a path of mastery or peace.

To know the self is not to build an identity around ego or biography, but to perceive clearly the layers of our being:

- **Physical:** Our body is the vessel through which we act, train, and endure. It must be honored and developed—not just for performance, but for longevity and resilience.

- **Mental:** Our thoughts form the lens through which we interpret the world. Clear thinking, discipline, and reflection refine this lens.

- **Spiritual**: Beyond the surface lies our true essence—a spark of the divine. The spirit speaks not in words but in knowing, in clarity, in conscience.

- **Relational**: Who we are is tested in how we treat others. Our ability to relate, uplift, forgive, and empathize shows our inner cultivation.

Delusion, what some ancient teachers referred to as *Doe Chi*, is the state of mistaking the unreal for the real. It blinds us to cause and consequence, to truth and error. To overcome delusion, we must ask deeply, *"Who am I, beneath the conditioning, titles, and emotions?"* In that honest inquiry, we begin to awaken.

3. True Living: Learn and Earn

"To live is to learn; to give is to earn." These are not just poetic phrases, but spiritual principles embedded in the structure of life itself.
- **Learning** requires humility, curiosity, and courage. It involves making mistakes and growing from them, not with guilt, but with gratitude.
- **Earning** in this tradition is not material wealth, but spiritual currency. It is the impact you leave, the good you sow, the wisdom you pass on.

A meaningful life demands that we move beyond consumption and toward contribution. As one ancient story teaches: the candle that lights another does not lose its flame. In fact, in giving light, its purpose is fulfilled.

True living is cyclical: we *learn* through inner work and discipline, and we *earn* by serving, teaching, and healing. Every act of kindness, clarity, or courage becomes a seed that may take root in others, and often in ways we will never see.

Building the Inner Temple

4. Be Your Own Guard

Guarding the mind and body is among the most sacred duties on the path. Just as a temple has a gate and guardian, so must our lives be protected from corrupting forces. This does not mean being closed or rigid. It means remaining clear, discerning, and grounded.

There are three "fathers" in a person's life: the divine or spiritual source (God), our biological fathers, and our mentors or teachers. Each plays a unique and non-replaceable role in our formation. Together, they form a triangle of head, heart, and feet, guiding us with wisdom, care, and direction.

To be your own guard is to:

- Examine what enters your mind through media, speech, and environment.
- Protect your body with appropriate physical movement, rest, nutrition, and breath.
- Guard your spirit through faith, purpose, and principle.

Teach your family to build these boundaries too. Children are shaped by what they see and what they're allowed to invite in. A home that is too open invites chaos, and a home too closed stifles growth. Invisible, energetic boundaries are sacred, they guide the flow of life without control.

5. Teach with Wisdom

Teaching is not merely about transferring information. It is about transforming lives. A true teacher is not only an expert in a subject, but a master of their own emotions, ego, and purpose.

The eight traits of a wisdom-based teacher are:

- **Vision** – Sees what is possible in the student even before they do.
- **Mastery** – Demonstrates embodied knowledge.
- **Discernment** – Knows when to challenge and when to support.
- **Leadership** – Models the way forward.
- **Compassion** – Meets students with patience and care.
- **Wisdom** – Connects teaching to life's deeper lessons.

- **Loyalty** – Holds commitment to the student's true growth.
- **Persistence** – Continues through difficulty.

The teacher becomes a "third parent" as a moral guide and spiritual compass. To earn this role, one must live the teachings, not just speak them. Real learning arises not through pressure, but through clarity and demonstration.

6. Build with Patience

Patience is not weakness. It is power held in stillness. It arises from vision: when we can see the outcome ahead, we are less likely to rush or force progress. Just as a seed takes time to sprout, and a bridge must be measured before it is built, so too must our work be prepared with care.

We must ask:

- What is the structure I'm building?
- When is the right season to begin?
- What foundation must be in place first?

True patience is not inertia. It is intentional pause. It is restraint guided by readiness. It trusts the process and honors the timing of nature and spirit.

7. Seek Correct Understanding

Many conflicts arise not from malice, but from misunderstanding. Right understanding is the foundation of right action. It is how we prevent needless suffering, restore broken relationships, and build wisdom.

Understanding requires more than hearing. It requires presence, inquiry, and alignment.

Eight methods to increase understanding:

1. **Speak eye to eye** – Engagement builds clarity.
2. **Ask if uncertain** – Clarify before assuming.
3. **Observe details** – Truth hides in what is subtle.
4. **Focus deeply** – Distraction distorts comprehension.
5. **Treat communication as sacred** – Words shape energy.
6. **Lead into calmness** – A quiet heart hears more.

7. **Encourage upward thinking** – Raise conversations toward growth.

8. **Use relevant examples** – Stories clarify the abstract.

True understanding bridges difference. It neutralizes judgment. It becomes the foundation upon which all healing and transformation can take place

Walking the Way

8. Avoid Seeking Attention

Those who seek constant validation or recognition are often covering deeper wounds like fear of invisibility, insecurity, or a lack of self-worth. But the more one chases attention, the more elusive it becomes. Like chasing your own shadow, the pursuit can never satisfy.

True strength is quiet, still, and radiant. It doesn't demand notice because it carries its own presence. To do good and walk away from the need for praise is one of the highest forms of mastery.

Boasting, complaining, dramatic behavior, or false humility are signs of imbalance. Attention seekers are often disconnected from their roots and rely on others to confirm their value. The one who is aligned with principle does not need applause as they are nourished by their integrity.

The corrective to attention-seeking is contrast: do the right thing in silence. Be the calm one in the storm. Offer light when others bring heat. Let your actions reflect the teaching, not your words.

"An empty can often makes the most noise." Cultivate substance over sound.

9. Think Correctly, Avoid Foolishness

Right thinking is the engine behind right living. But modern life often encourages impulsive, shallow, or distracted thought. To live wisely, we must reclaim the art of thinking long, wide, and deep.

- **Long** thinking asks: What are the long-term consequences of this choice?

- **Wide** thinking asks: How will this affect others, not just myself?

- **Deep** thinking asks: What is the truest, most aligned reason behind this action?

Foolishness often appears as overconfidence, stubbornness, or mental laziness. The fool is not someone without knowledge, but someone who ignores feedback, resists growth, and speaks more than they listen.

Correct thinking is quiet and layered. It builds discernment and avoids extremes. Wisdom is not found in being right all the time, but in knowing when to pause, re-evaluate, and correct your path.

The world needs fewer clever people and more wise ones.

10. Respond as a Person of Balance

A balanced individual is not free from conflict, but however they are free from chaos within. They can see events, people, and even insults with space around them. They don't absorb every emotion or overreact to every situation.

Balance is not apathy. It is strength under control. It is action shaped by awareness. When provoked, the balanced person does not explode or collapse. They assess. They adjust. They move with grounded responsiveness.

Even when imbalance arises, as it does for all of us, a trained mind will return to center faster. Like a tree that sways but does not break.

The main causes of imbalance include:

- **Misunderstanding** – Assumptions that lead to false conclusions.

- **Anger** – Often a signal of unmet needs or unresolved hurt.

- **Fear** – A disconnect from trust and clarity.

Training for balance is a lifelong process. It comes through breathwork, reflection, martial discipline, relational harmony, and spiritual clarity. While perfect balance may elude us in this lifetime, the pursuit itself makes us more whole.

Balance is not a destination, but rather it is a way of being.

The Living Legacy

11. Leave Behind Good Seeds

A meaningful life is not defined by possessions, achievements, or popularity. It is defined by the quiet seeds we plant in the lives of others. These seeds are our words, our actions, our sacrifices, and our presence. Some bloom quickly; others lie dormant until a moment of need. But every genuine seed sown in truth, kindness, and clarity will take root in time.

Honor, wisdom, courage, and peace are invisible treasures. Uncharted on maps and untouched by inflation or decay. The *Path of Integrity* invites us to benefit from such treasures in our homes, relationships, communities, and disciplines.

By contrast, the *Way of Dissonance* leaves behind resentment, broken trust, and regret. This, too, is a legacy, but one that burdens future generations. Choose consciously which inheritance your footsteps will leave.

Ask yourself daily: Are my thoughts planting harmony or discord? Are my words seeds of encouragement or erosion? Am I sowing actions that bring light?

True immortality lies not in prolonging life, but in multiplying good through others.

12. Seek the Face of Honor

Honor is not a performance. It is not something others bestow. It is who we are when no one is watching. To live with honor is to align one's behavior with truth, one's spirit with principle, and one's legacy with integrity.

In a world of shifting masks and performative virtue, the face of honor remains unchanged. It is steady, dignified, and humble. It seeks no recognition but is recognized by all. To *"seek the face of honor"* is to pursue a state of being that reflects what is eternal in us.

Honor connects us to our root, or our deepest nature. Without it, we drift, unsure of who we are or where we belong. With it, we walk clearly, even through confusion.

True honor uplifts. It inspires others to rise without tearing anyone down. It is expressed through consistency, accountability, respect, and service.

Surround yourself with people who live this way. Become someone who restores it in others.

13. Change Your Reality

Your life is not a fixed script, but more like a canvas. The brush is your awareness, the paint, your thoughts, beliefs, and decisions. To walk the Warrior-Scholar-Sage path is to realize that you are both the artist and the art.

Reality changes when perception changes. This does not mean ignoring difficulties or living in denial. It means choosing how to meet life with empowered vision. You are not at the mercy of fate. You shape it through:

- **Discernment** – knowing what is true, even when it's unpopular.
- **Self-discipline** – mastering your time, speech, and effort.
- **Meditation** – hearing the quiet guidance within.
- **Internal cultivation** – training breath, energy, movement, and spirit.

Ancient traditions have always taught this power. They spoke in metaphors: the alchemist, the sage, the inner fire. But the message is the same. You can transform your state from confusion to clarity, from reaction to creation.

Begin not with the world, but with yourself. That is where the turning begins.

14. Become a Living Vessel of Wisdom

Wisdom is not something we acquire once and for all. It flows, it grows, it humbles us. It only enters when the ego exits. To become a living vessel of wisdom is to allow timeless truth to pass through you into the lives of others.

A vessel is not defined by its decoration, but by its capacity and what it contains. Make yourself worthy to carry wisdom by emptying yourself of ego, fear, and need for status.

Wisdom does not seek applause. Rather it seeks application. It is known for its fruit: peace, clarity, service, and the elevation of others.

A vessel must also be strong. Wisdom, if not grounded in discipline and resilience, can be distorted by pride. Thus, the way of wisdom is the way of balance. Open, but not naive; clear, but not rigid.

15. Inner Cultivation: The Inner Art of Vitality

True strength comes not from muscle alone, but from the integration of breath, awareness, movement, and energy. Inner cultivation is the ancient and evolving art of aligning one's life force, what the Chinese call *qi,* with intention and harmony. Wind and water makes fire.

Three elemental principles guide this path:

- **Wind (Breath / Bagua)** – Movement and transformation, guiding adaptability and insight.

- **Water (Movement / Tai Chi)** – Flow, softness, resilience, and the wisdom of yielding.

- **Fire (Qi / Qigong)** – Energy, willpower, and the circulation of internal power.

Practices like Qigong, BaguaZhang, and Tai Chi are not just exercises. They are disciplines of refinement. They reconnect us with natural law. They balance the nervous system, strengthen immunity, clear emotional stagnation, and sharpen focus.

From stillness to flow, from breath to intention, this path teaches us how to not only survive, but to thrive with grace, presence, and inner light.

16. The Seed of Peace

The mind is ever-changing, like a leaf on a stream. Left unchecked, it flows wherever the current takes it: reacting to fears, drawn to distraction, swayed by noise. But with principle, the mind finds its anchor. And with stillness, the spirit begins to speak.

Inside every human being is a seed of peace. It is not manufactured; it is remembered. It lives beneath the layers of stress, history, and fear. It cannot be forced to grow. It must be nourished. The nourishment is sincerity. Water is awareness. The light is spiritual discipline.

The *Path of Integrity* is not about perfection. It is about persistence. Each day, we falter and recalibrate. Each moment offers us the chance to return. To return to principle, to root, to stillness.

To follow the Warrior-Scholar-Sage path is not to remove oneself from life, but to engage life with presence, wisdom, and purpose. We are here to learn, to guide, to transform. And ultimately, to radiate the peace we have cultivated within.

When the mind leads without enlightenment, there is confusion. When your spirit leads with humility and clarity, there is peace.

Let your life become a vessel through which that seed of peace is shared with a world deeply in need of it.

SECTION II: ESSAYS

A: Spiritual Paradoxes & Theological Reflections

Spiritual Paradoxes: Humility Taught, Materialism Practiced

Across time and cultures, the greatest spiritual teachers have emphasized simplicity, humility, and inner transformation. Yet, paradoxically, the institutions that grow around these teachings often accumulate material wealth, political power, and ego-driven prestige.
Christianity, Buddhism, Hinduism, Islam, all at their core, advocate for the shedding of worldly attachments. Yet many of their largest institutions exhibit the very materialism and hierarchy their founders warned against. In light of today's cultural unrest, consumerism, and spiritual seeking, these contradictions deserve closer reflection.

A Humble Beginning

Jesus of Nazareth lived with radical humility. His birth in a manger (Luke 2:7, New International Version [NIV]), his itinerant lifestyle (*"the Son of Man has no place to lay his head,"* Luke 9:58, NIV), and his repeated critiques of religious legalism (Matthew 23:1–28, NIV) demonstrate a clear rejection of material power and ritualized pretense.
He warned against storing up treasures on earth, urging people instead to seek spiritual treasures (Matthew 6:19–21, NIV). His message was direct: inner transformation and compassion mattered more than public ritual or personal gain.

And yet, centuries later, the Roman Catholic Church emerged from the very empire that crucified him, to became one of the wealthiest and most ritualized institutions in human history (MacCulloch, 2011).

A Universal Paradox

This irony is not exclusive to Christianity. It is a universal pattern across major belief systems:

- **Buddhism**: Siddhartha Gautama, the Buddha, renounced his royal status to seek enlightenment through simplicity and meditation. His core teaching of the elimination of craving and attachment became institutionalized into monasteries and sects, some of which, over centuries, accumulated wealth, political influence, and hierarchical authority (Lopez, 2001).

- **Hinduism**: Early Vedic teachings stressed detachment from material life through paths like *Jnana* (knowledge) and *Bhakti* (devotion). Yet, sprawling temple complexes, priestly hierarchies, and caste structures often mirrored societal materialism and status-seeking (Flood, 1996).

- **Islam**: The Prophet Muhammad lived simply, called for humility, and emphasized equality among believers. Yet throughout history, caliphates and modern regimes alike have at times entangled faith with vast political and material ambitions (Esposito, 1998).

Again and again, humanity seems to be drawn to codify spiritual simplicity into worldly complexity.

Why Does This Happen?

From a psychological and sociological standpoint, this paradox might stem from natural human tendencies:

- **Desire for Security**: Spiritual communities often accumulate resources to protect their teachings and communities from external threats.

- **Institutionalization**: Movements grow into organizations, and organizations seek stability, leading to bureaucracy and hierarchy.

- **Human Ego**: Even with the best intentions, individuals and groups may seek recognition, authority, and influence, contradicting the original teachings.

As the Tao Te Ching observes, *"The higher the structure, the farther from the Way"* (Laozi, trans. Mitchell, 1988).

Cultural Relevance Today

Today's society, riddled with consumerism, curated self-images, and institutional distrust, mirrors these spiritual paradoxes. Many seekers are disillusioned with religious structures not because they reject faith, but because they crave *authenticity*.

Holistic health practitioners recognize that wellness is found in true balance of mind, body, and spirit, and requires stripping away external noise and realigning with essential truths. It's not in grandeur but in simplicity that healing often occurs.

The example of figures like Jesus, Buddha, and Muhammad calls us back not to ritualized identity, but to the living essence of humility, compassion, and conscious living.

A Personal Reflection

This reflection isn't a condemnation of all spiritual institutions. Rather, it is a call to vigilance:

- Are we aligning with the heart of spiritual wisdom or merely its outer forms?
- Are we living simply, authentically, and compassionately, or becoming entangled in ego, status, and recognition?

As individuals seeking holistic well-being, we are invited to live in *the spirit* rather than merely follow *the form*.

Spiritual maturity requires discernment and choosing the inward journey over external display, whether in religion, health, or daily life.

References:

Esposito, J. L. (1998). *Islam: The straight path* (3rd ed.). Oxford University Press.

Flood, G. (1996). *An introduction to Hinduism*. Cambridge University Press.

Lopez, D. S., Jr. (2001). *THE STORY OF BUDDHISM*. HarperSanFrancisco. http://www.chanreads.org/wp-content/uploads/2022/09/The-Story-of-Buddhism-A-Concise-Guide-to-Its-History-Teachings-Donald-S.-Lopez-Jr.-chanreads.org_.pdf

MacCulloch, D. (2011). *Christianity: The first three thousand years*. Penguin Books.

Mitchell, S. (Trans.). (1988). *Tao Te Ching* (Lao Tzu). Harper & Row.

The Holy Bible, New International Version. (2011). Biblica, Inc. (Original work published 1978)

Do We Die and Go to Heaven, or Die and Bring Heaven with Us?

Many say they know of the afterlife either being a good place (heaven) or a bad place (hell). Others believe that life here is a temporary classroom, where we keep coming back to revisiting lessons not yet understood. No one alive can truly know the proven existence of any life beyond their current physical manifestation. Some hope for an afterlife that is heavenly but also live a life that is hellish. Quite the quandary, no?

Why not try to live a heavenly life, and hopefully bring that with you when you pass? It sounds better than living in hell on earth and then taking hell with you to the next level of existence. There are many theories regarding the laws of attraction and how we often acquire what we dwell upon, whether deemed as good or bad. Those who think mainly about wealth and/or fame put much of their energy into obtaining these things. However, once they acquire these items, they often realize that they are not truly happy with themselves because they sacrificed things such as family, friends, health, and other aspects of their being.

Others see God's kingdom as heaven on earth. Their life may be full of love, gratitude, and happiness. Some may see their physical life here on earth as hell, with none of the previously mentioned aspects, and therefore look forward to hopefully reaching a better place in the hereafter. The famous philosopher Confucius is thought to have said that we should not focus on the afterlife because we don't understand much about it. Instead, we should focus on our everyday life here in the present.

I take this further to mean that we can choose to believe that the Kingdom of God is here right now, in our mind and body, here in the physical world. My understanding is that the state of our thoughts at the very time of our passing is of the utmost importance. What we do or don't do here on Earth within our physical lifetimes can and will affect what happens to our soul or consciousness after our physical being expires.

I have personally been exposed to many people who are most concerned about what may happen in their next life, with very little concern about how they live this current physical life. Others care only about their wants and desires in front of them, with no concerns about what may come next. We may indeed die and go to a place of heaven or hell based upon how we live our lives. If we strive to live a "heavenly-like" life, we may be able to take that peacefulness, joy, and bliss with us to whatever the next phase we have earned. Conversely, if we live a life full of hell in anger, hatred, suffering, and regret, we very well may bring that negative energy to whatever that next place may be.

If Jesus Returned Today

A Holistic Look at Faith, Skepticism, and the Human Response to the Divine

Easter is one of the most widely celebrated religious holidays across the globe, observed by billions of people through both spiritual and cultural traditions. For Christians, it commemorates the resurrection of Jesus Christ, an event central to the faith and steeped in mystery, reverence, and awe. Yet, when we peel back the layers of devotion and ritual, deeper questions arise:

- What exactly happened leading up to the crucifixion?
- Why did Jesus die?
- If Jesus were alive today, would He be embraced or dismissed as a fraud?
- Would He be celebrated or condemned all over again?

These questions may seem theological at first glance, but they also probe into human psychology, sociology, and the nature of our collective consciousness. Let's explore this landscape more fully.

The Life and Death of Jesus: A Brief Chronology

The crucifixion of Jesus was not a random act of violence but the culmination of escalating tension. His teachings challenged the religious elite and threatened both Roman and Jewish political structures. Betrayed by Judas Iscariot, arrested in the Garden of Gethsemane, and denied three times by Peter, Jesus was ultimately condemned, scourged, and crucified under Roman law.

According to the Gospels, He died a slow, excruciating death, most likely from a combination of blood loss, asphyxiation, and shock. His body was placed in a tomb, and yet, three days later, reports of His resurrection spread. For the next 40 days, Jesus appeared to His disciples and followers in various places, teaching and preparing them before ascending into heaven.

But His post-resurrection appearances were not always public or easily verified, likely to avoid immediate conflict with His enemies. This subtle presence helped build the early Christian movement without triggering another wave of persecution, yet it also raises timeless questions.

Would Jesus Be Accepted Today?

Imagine Jesus walking the Earth today, preaching love, repentance, and divine truth. Would He be revered? Or ridiculed?

For many devout Christians, His return is not only expected but deeply hoped for. But it's also possible that His reappearance would challenge modern religious institutions, political ideologies, and cultural norms. His radical message of loving enemies, renouncing materialism, forgiving unconditionally, and living humbly runs counter to consumer culture, tribalism, and vengeance-based systems of justice.

In a secular and scientific age, He might be dismissed as delusional, cult-like, or mentally unstable. Social media would amplify both the adoration and the condemnation. News outlets would scrutinize every word. Authorities might intervene. Even some who claim to follow Him might not recognize Him if He failed to fit their expectations.

Miracles, Demons, and the Modern Lens

Jesus' time was filled with accounts of miracles such as healing the sick, calming storms, walking on water, and casting out demons. But how do we interpret those today?

It's worth asking: were demon possessions more common in antiquity, or was there simply a lack of medical and psychological understanding? Conditions we now label as epilepsy, schizophrenia, or PTSD may have once been seen through a spiritual lens. That doesn't necessarily disprove the spiritual dimension, it just reminds us that knowledge evolves, and perception is always shaped by context.

Many ancient cultures viewed health holistically, body, mind, and spirit as inseparable. In that light, Jesus' healing work can still be seen as deeply integrative, restoring not just physical health, but emotional, mental, and spiritual balance.

Do People Still Celebrate Easter as a Religious Holiday?

In the United States, Easter remains a significant holiday, but often more as a cultural celebration than a sacred observance. About 81% of Americans celebrate Easter (Statista, 2025), but only around 30% attend religious services (Jones, 2025). For many, Easter involves candy, egg hunts, spring fashion, and family meals more than deep spiritual reflection.

Globally, however, Easter remains a central pillar for over two billion Christians, and even those who don't consider themselves religious often participate in its communal and festive traditions.

The Pattern of Human Response to Visionaries

Jesus was not the only historical figure to be rejected in His time and revered later. In fact, history repeats itself with uncanny regularity:

Figure	During Their Life	Now Remembered As
Jesus Christ	Executed as a criminal and heretic	Savior, Son of God, Redeemer
Socrates	Sentenced to death for corrupting the youth	Father of Western Philosophy
Martin Luther King Jr.	Monitored and opposed; assassinated	Civil Rights Icon
Joan of Arc	Burned at the stake for heresy	Catholic Saint and French Heroine
Galileo Galilei	Placed under house arrest for scientific beliefs	Father of Modern Science
Nelson Mandela	Imprisoned as a dissident	Global Symbol of Peace and Freedom

Figure	During Their Life	Now Remembered As
Mother Teresa	Criticized and praised	Canonized Saint and Humanitarian

This pattern teaches us something vital: those who carry truth, challenge norms, or disrupt unjust systems are often rejected in their own time, only to be honored by future generations once the world has caught up.

Final Reflection

If Jesus Christ were to return today, not as a celebrity preacher or political figure, but as the humble, radical healer Jesus was, there's a strong chance he would face the same resistance that he did 2,000 years ago.

Yet, the holistic view reminds us that truth transcends time. While forms change, principles remain. Whether we view Jesus through a spiritual, symbolic, or historical lens, His life challenges us to look inward, to seek compassion, and to live from the soul rather than the ego.

The deeper question isn't whether the world would accept Jesus, but whether we would recognize Him in our own lives, our own thoughts, and the strangers we encounter daily.

References:

Statista. (2025, March 3). *Share of Americans celebrating Easter from 2009-2023*. https://www.statista.com/statistics/221108/share-of-americans-celebrating-easter-since-2007/

Jones, B. J. M. (2025, March 26). Church attendance has declined in most U.S. religious groups. Gallup.com. https://news.gallup.com/poll/642548/church-attendance-declined-religious-groups.aspx?utm_source=chatgpt.com

The Conscious Exploiter: When Awareness Replaces Gratitude

In human relationships, it is natural to give and to hope that our giving is met with acknowledgment, respect, or at the very least basic appreciation. But what happens when someone receives generously, with full awareness of the giver's effort or sacrifice, yet responds with silence, indifference, or calculated detachment?

This is the subtle, unsettling behavior of what we may call a **conscious exploiter.** A person who takes with mindfulness but withholds gratitude by choice.

Unlike the oblivious or socially inept, the conscious exploiter is often intellectually aware and emotionally capable but operates with an internal moral economy that excludes reciprocation. Their mindset resembles a form of calculated opportunism, wherein taking becomes justified through rationalizations, entitlements, or social positioning. As psychologist George Simon explains in *In Sheep's Clothing* (2010), manipulative personalities often know what they're doing but frame their actions to appear innocent or justified, making their ingratitude seem subtle or even acceptable (Simon, 2010).

Gratitude as a Marker of Moral Awareness

Gratitude is more than a polite gesture; it's a sign of mutual recognition, emotional intelligence, and social maturity. Psychologist Robert Emmons, a leading researcher in gratitude science, describes it as "a relationship-strengthening emotion" that connects giver and receiver in a mutual bond of awareness (Emmons & McCullough, 2003). When someone consciously receives but fails to show appreciation, they break the cycle of relational reciprocity, often creating emotional imbalance and mistrust.

Yet in modern society, especially in competitive environments or hierarchical communities, this behavior can become normalized. When success or advantage is prioritized above virtue, even intelligent and aware individuals may suppress expressions of gratitude to maintain power, status, or detachment.

The Ethical Cost of Calculated Ingratitude

From a philosophical lens, this conduct undermines ethical living. The Stoics, such as Seneca, warned of taking without gratitude as a sign of moral decline, arguing that "he who receives a benefit with gratitude repays the first installment on his debt" (*On Benefits*, trans. Basore, 1935). In Taoist tradition, the natural flow of energy (or *qi*) depends on balance and reciprocity, not unilateral absorption. To receive while withholding thanks is to disrupt the harmonious flow that underpins healthy relationships.

Such individuals may outwardly maintain charm, social grace, or even spiritual language, but their inner posture remains self-serving. They are *"courteous faces masking consuming hearts,"* quietly draining emotional resources from those around them.

Recognizing the Pattern

The conscious exploiter is not always easy to identify. Their ingratitude is not loud; it is quiet, measured, and often cloaked in charisma or deflection. You may notice:

- They accept help readily but never inquire about your well-being.
- They benefit from your time, knowledge, or effort, yet leave without acknowledgment.
- They strategically maintain relationships that serve their needs, but dissolve or ignore those that ask for emotional investment.

Unlike the unaware, these individuals choose not to give back. Not out of inability, but out of intention.

Healing the Pattern

For those affected by such dynamics, healing begins with clear boundaries, conscious awareness, and a return to self-honoring. Recognize the signs not with bitterness, but with clarity. You are not obliged to pour into vessels that give nothing in return. As spiritual teacher

Gabor Maté emphasizes, boundaries are not walls, but necessary structures to protect your energy and values (Maté, 2022).

References:

- Emmons, R. A., & McCullough, M. E. (2003). Counting blessings versus burdens: An experimental investigation of gratitude and subjective well-being in daily life. *Journal of Personality and Social Psychology, 84*(2), 377–389. https://doi.org/10.1037/0022-3514.84.2.377
- Maté, G. (2022). *The Myth of Normal: Trauma, Illness & Healing in a Toxic Culture*. Avery.
- Seneca L. (1935). *On Benefits* (trans. Aubrey Stewart & E.H. Warmington, Loeb Classical Library). Harvard University Press.
- Simon, G. (2010). *In Sheep's Clothing: Understanding and Dealing with Manipulative People*. Parkhurst Brothers Publishers.

The Upside-Down King: A Lesson in Humility, Wisdom, and True Power

The Chinese character for humility is 谦 (qiān). The character for a king (or ruler) is 王 (wáng), but when flipped, it can be associated with something reversed, such as a reversed position, or lack of power. Combining these, one could interpret 谦王 (qiān wáng) as "humble ruler" or "modest king", representing a ruler who is both powerful and humble.

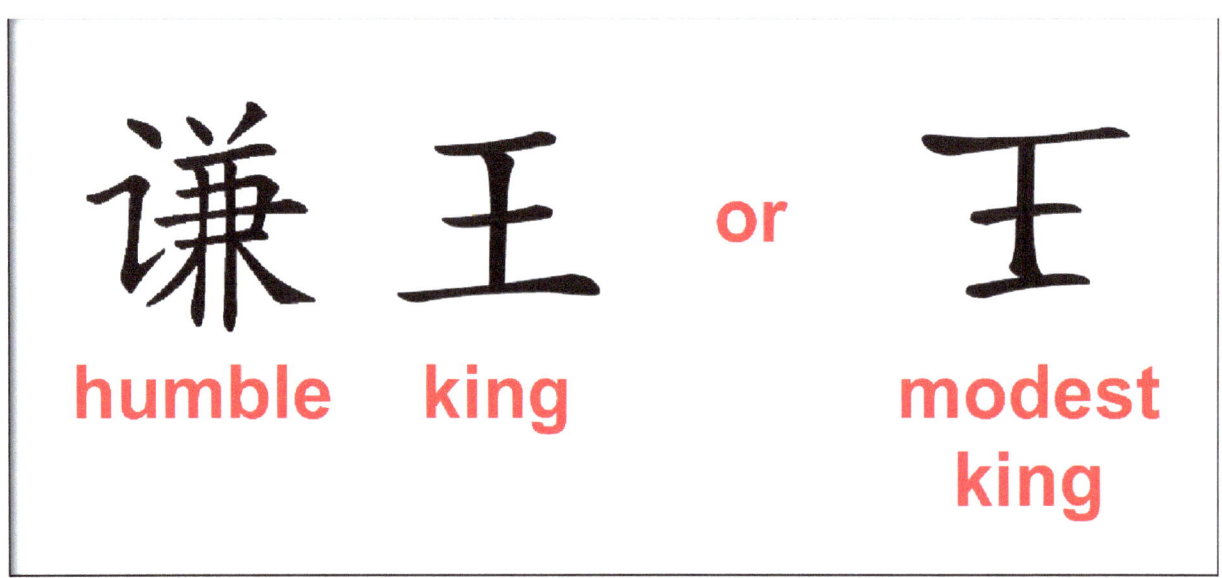

In a time long ago, a great king ruled over a vast and prosperous land. Despite his power, he felt something was missing. Perhaps an imbalance in the heart of his kingdom and perhaps within himself. Recognizing the limits of his own understanding, the king invited a wise man to help restore harmony to his realm.

The wise man accepted the invitation, bringing with him not armies or gold, but clarity, insight, and timeless wisdom. Through thoughtful guidance, he realigned the kingdom's priorities. Not by conquering enemies, but by restoring balance between the people and their values. He offered no lectures on dominance or strategy, but instead taught the king to listen more, act less, and lead from within. And then, without asking for any reward or recognition, the wise man quietly departed.

The king was stunned. He had expected a request for treasure or title. Instead, the king was left with only the echo of wisdom that had shifted the foundation of his being. He was no longer the same man. In honor of this transformative experience, the king ordered the Chinese character for "king" (王) to be turned upside down wherever it appeared in his palace.

This symbolic act was not a rejection of power, but rather a redefinition of it. By inverting the symbol of his own authority, the king declared a new truth:

Wisdom is greater than power. Humility is the highest throne.

The Deeper Meaning
While the tale may not be part of the classic canon of Chinese folklore, its message is deeply rooted in Eastern philosophy and holistic wisdom traditions.

In **Taoist** thought, the greatest rulers are often those who lead without force. The sage governs by aligning with the *Tao* or natural order, practicing *wu wei* or effortless action, and allowing things to unfold organically.

In **Confucian** ethics, the moral character of the ruler sets the tone for the nation. A wise and virtuous leader brings peace not through decrees but by embodying righteousness.

In **Buddhist** teachings, detachment from ego and recognition of impermanence guide the wise. Like the sage in the story, the Bodhisattva acts for the benefit of others without seeking personal gain.

The upside-down character becomes a living reminder: true power lies not in domination, but in service, awareness, and the willingness to learn.

A Reflection for Our Times

In today's world, where leadership is often equated with control, and success with status, the *Upside-Down King* offers us a timeless teaching:

Sometimes, the greatest transformation comes not from gaining more, but from surrendering pride and embracing wisdom.

This story reminds us that holistic well-being begins with humility, whether we are leading others, caring for our health, or walking the path of self-discovery. The body may follow orders, but the soul responds to truth. And in the realm of wellness, just as in the kingdom of the wise king, balance is restored when wisdom reigns over ego.

B: Eastern Philosophy, Metaphysics & Inner Alchemy

From Wuji to Tai Chi

Understanding the Evolution of Supreme Principles in Daoist Cosmology

In the study of Daoist philosophy and traditional Chinese thought, the term "Tai Chi" (太極) is widely recognized as referring to the **Supreme Ultimate**, a foundational principle in the universe from which all dualities (*yin* and *yang*) arise (Liao,1990).

Practitioners of Tai Chi Chuan may know the term as associated with martial arts, yet its roots are far deeper, embedded in cosmology, metaphysics, and classical Daoist thought. But what if we go one step earlier, or even further back? What came before Tai Chi? And what of other similarly constructed terms such as ***"Tai Su"*** (太素) and ***"Tai Yu"*** (太宇)? Are they simply linguistic variants, or do they represent unique philosophical concepts in the evolution of universal principles?

Wuji (無極): The Limitless Void

In the beginning was **Wuji**, often translated as "non-ultimate" or "limitless." Wuji represents pure potential being formless, timeless, and undivided. It is the **Dao** before manifestation (Robinet, 1997). In diagrams, Wuji is usually shown as an empty circle or a vast blank space, signifying the absence of polarity.

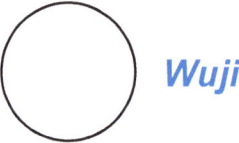
Wuji

Tai Su (太素): The Supreme Simplicity

Emerging from Wuji is **Tai Su**, a term less commonly discussed but highly significant in classical Daoist texts.

- **Tai (太)** = supreme or great
- **Su (素)** = simple, elemental, unadorned, or fundamental substance

Tai Su is understood as the primordial essence or supreme simplicity. A state where differentiation is beginning to arise but not yet fully formed. It is the first stirring of substance, the bridge between the void and duality. In *Huainanzi*, Tai Su is mentioned as a precursor to cosmic formation (Le Blanc & Mathieu, 2008). In early Chinese alchemy and cosmology, it represents the primordial *qi* that has yet to divide into yin and yang (Pregadio, 2008).

Simplicity

Tai Chi (太極): The Supreme Ultimate

When differentiation occurs, **Tai Chi** comes into being. The term, often Romanized as **Taiji**, literally means **"Supreme Ultimate."** This is the phase where the one becomes two: yin and yang emerge as complementary polarities (Liao,1990).

Tai Chi is typically symbolized by the **Taijitu**, the black-and-white "yin-yang" symbol, expressing balance, transformation, and interdependence. In this state, movement and stillness alternate, giving rise to all forms in the universe (Kirkland, 2004).

Taiiitu

Tai Yu (太宇): The Supreme Universe

Tai Yu introduces a more spatial or structural aspect to cosmology.

- **Yu (宇)** refers to the universe, cosmic space, or even the eaves of a roof, or a poetic image of a sheltering order.
- Thus, Tai Yu translates to "Supreme Universe" or "Great Cosmos."

While Tai Chi marks the origin of dynamic duality, Tai Yu is more about manifested order, and the structured universe as it exists with stars, planets, natural laws, and cycles (Graham, 1989). It is not a transitional phase but the result of the Tai Chi mechanism unfolding through space and time.

Cosmological Sequence Diagram

To visualize this progression, the accompanying diagram illustrates the unfolding of the cosmos:

1. **Wuji (無極)** – The Limitless Void

    ↓

2. **Tai Su (太素)** – Supreme Simplicity (undifferentiated essence)

    ↓

3. **Tai Chi (太極)** – Supreme Ultimate (birth of yin and yang)

↓

4. **Tai Yu (太宇)** – Supreme Universe (structured cosmos)

Term	Translation	Symbol	Meaning
Wuji	Limitless Void	Empty circle (○)	Undifferentiated nothingness
Tai Su	Supreme Simplicity	Solid black circle (●)	Primordial essence
Tai Chi	Supreme Ultimate	Yin-Yang (☯ / Taijitu)	Birth of duality
Tai Yu	Supreme Universe	Bagua or Heaven–Earth (八卦 / 天地)	Manifest cosmos; structured reality

Cultural and Linguistic Notes: Korean Equivalents

In Korean, these terms are written in Hanja (Chinese characters used in Korean language):

- **Tai Chi (太極)** ⟶ **Tae Guk (태극)**, as seen in the South Korean flag

- **Tai Su (太素)** ⟶ **Tae So (태소)** (rarely used in common language)

- **Tai Yu (太宇)** ⟶ **Tae U (태우)** (used in poetic or classical references)

While the philosophical usage remains mostly consistent with Chinese meanings, these terms are far less prevalent in Korean popular culture outside of Tae Guk.

Conclusion: A Philosophical Framework of Evolution

From non-being to primordial essence, and from dynamic polarity to cosmic order, this cosmological sequence illustrates how Daoist philosophy views the evolution of the universe not as a chaotic explosion, but as an elegant, cyclical, and ordered unfolding.

Whether you are a practitioner of martial arts, a student of Daoist metaphysics, or a philosopher of natural laws, understanding **Wuji** ⟶ **Tai Su** ⟶ **Tai Chi** ⟶ **Tai Yu** offers a powerful lens through which to view the origin of all things and your own place within the ever-unfolding Tao.

Important to note, in martial arts culture, Tai chi, Tai Su, Tai Yu, Tae Guk and Tai Chi Chung are all very different forms of mental, physical and spiritual practices. While some may share some similarities, anyone who has deeply studied and practiced these methods is aware of their varying nuances and complexities.

Term	Characters	Translation	Philosophical Meaning
Wuji	無極	Non-Ultimate / Limitless	The primordial void; pure potential without polarity
Tai Su	太素	Supreme Simplicity / Primordial Essence	Undifferentiated, fundamental matter—precursor to form and duality
Tai Chi	太極	Supreme Ultimate	The origin of duality (yin and yang); dynamic balance
Tai Yu	太宇	Supreme Universe / Great Cosmos	The structured universe or cosmic order that emerges after duality

References:

Blanc, C. L., & Mathieu, R. (2008). Approches critiques de la mythologie chinoise. https://doi.org/10.4000/books.pum.19027

Graham, A. C. (1989). *Disputers of the Tao: Philosophical Argument in Ancient China*. Open Court.

Kirkland, R. (2004). *Taoism: The Enduring Tradition*. Routledge.

Pregadio, F. (2008). The Encyclopedia of Taoism. Routledge.

Robinet, I. (1997). *Taoism: Growth of a Religion*. Stanford University Press.
Liao, W. (n.d.). T'ai chi classics. Shambhala. https://www.shambhala.com/t-ai-chi-classics.html

The Threefold Way: Society, Nature, and Self in Chinese Philosophy

For centuries, Chinese culture has been shaped by a triad of the philosophical systems of **Confucianism**, **Taoism**, and **Buddhism**. Though distinct in their teachings, they are often seen as complementary threads that weave together a balanced and meaningful life. Each offers a unique focus: Confucianism emphasizes harmony in society, Taoism seeks unity with nature, and Buddhism turns inward to liberate the self from suffering (Yao, 2000).

Buddhism   **Taoism**   **Confucianism**

Confucianism: The Order of Society

Founded by Confucius (Kong Fuzi) around the 5th century BCE, Confucianism centers on ethics, duty, and the cultivation of virtuous behavior within a structured society. It promotes familial piety (*xiao*), respect for hierarchy, and the importance of education and ritual (*li*) (Sontag, 1974). A Confucian life is guided by the roles of the parent, child, ruler, subject, and the fulfillment of these roles builds a just and orderly world. It teaches that virtue in leadership trickles down to the moral development of the people (Yao, 2000).

Taoism: Flowing with Nature

Rooted in the *Tao Te Ching* by Laozi, Taoism (or Daoism) champions spontaneity, simplicity, and harmony with the *Tao,* or the ineffable force that flows through all things (Laozi, trans. Mitchell, 1988). Rather than striving to control or fix the world, the Taoist seeks to align with the natural order through non-resistance (*wu wei*), letting go of ego, and observing the rhythms of nature. Taoism speaks to the middle-aged soul, or one who questions structure and seeks authenticity and fluidity in life (Kirkland, 2004).

Buddhism: Awakening the Inner Self

Brought to China from India around the 1st century CE, Buddhism introduced a new inwardness, emphasizing meditation, compassion, and release from suffering through the Eightfold Path (Harvey, 2013). The Buddhist focus is not on society or external alignment but on awakening. It teaches that all phenomena are impermanent, and that liberation comes not from control or flow, but from transcending attachment entirely (Mitchell, 2002). In this way, Buddhism serves the aging soul by contemplating, detaching, and seeking ultimate freedom.

Integration: A Balanced Life

In traditional Chinese thought, these three paths were not meant to compete but to complete one another. A person might live as:
- *a Confucian in the office*

- *a Taoist in the garden*

- *a Buddhist in solitude* (Yao, 2000).

Together, they offer a map to live wisely with integrity in society, harmony in nature, and peace within the soul.

References:

Sontag, F. (1974). Herbert Fingarette. Confucius—the Secular as Sacred. (Harper and Row, New York, 1972.). *Religious Studies*, *10*(2), 245–246. https://doi.org/10.1017/s0034412500007514

Harvey, P. (2012). *An introduction to Buddhism.* https://doi.org/10.1017/cbo9781139050531

Taoism: the Enduring tradition. (n.d.). Routledge & CRC Press. https://www.routledge.com/Taoism-The-Enduring-Tradition/Kirkland/p/book/9780415263221?utm_source=cjaffiliates&utm_medium=affiliates&cjevent=eeb2c6c93e3c11f083ff00cf0a82b820

Mitchell, S. (1988). Tao Te Ching. In *HARPERPERENNIAL MODERNCLASSICS*. HARPERPERENNIAL MODERNCLASSICS. https://ia800904.us.archive.org/20/items/taoteching-Stephen-Mitchell-translation-v9deoq/taoteching-Stephen-Mitchell-translation-v9deoq_text.pdf

Mitchell, D. W. (2002). *Buddhism: Introducing the Buddhist experience.* Oxford University Press.

Yao, X. (2000). *An introduction to confucianism.* https://doi.org/10.1017/cbo9780511800887

The Buddhist Eightfold Path & the Taoist 8 Keys of Wisdom

*The **Eightfold Path*** in Buddhism and the ***Eight Keys of Wisdom*** both emphasize self-awareness, ethical living, and inner transformation, but they approach wisdom from different angles. Buddhism focuses on liberation from suffering and Taoism emphasizes harmony with the *Tao* (the Way). Below are summaries and correlations between them.

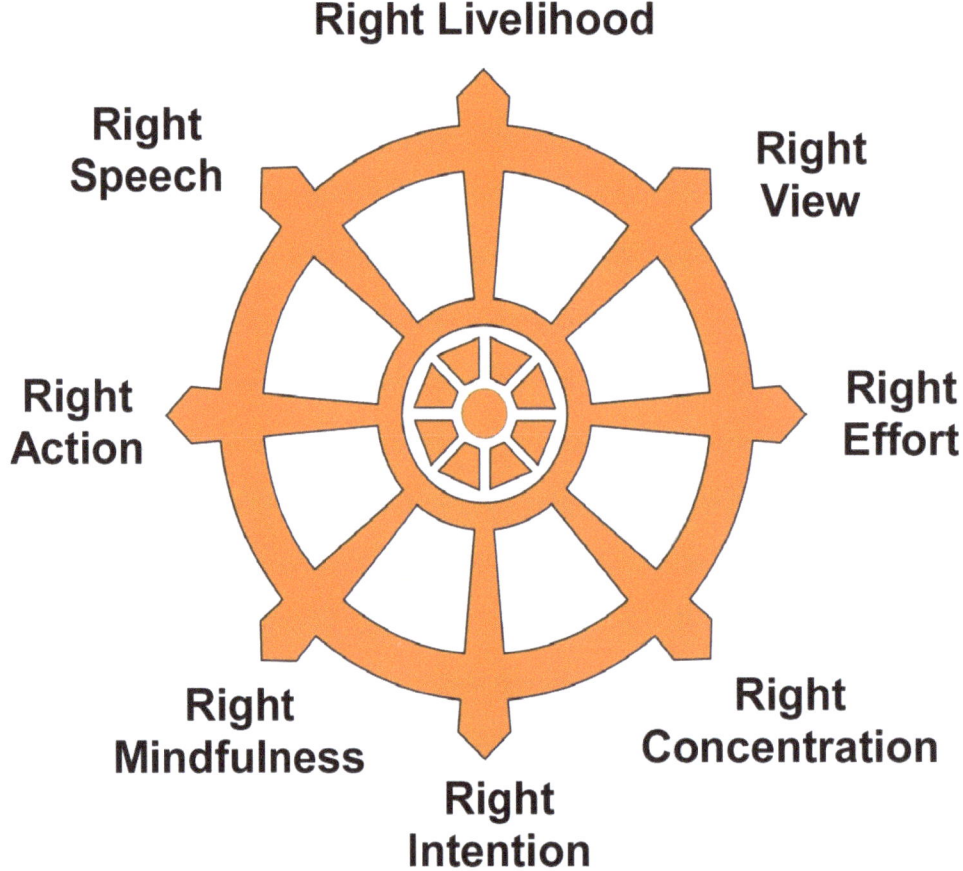

The **Buddhist Eightfold Path** is a core teaching of the Buddha, forming the practical aspect of the *Four Noble Truths*. It guides ethical conduct, mental discipline, and wisdom, leading to the cessation of suffering and enlightenment (*nirvana*).

The Eightfold Path consists of:
Wisdom (Prajñā / Panna)

1. **Right View (Sammā-diṭṭhi)** – Understanding the Four Noble Truths and seeing reality as it is.

2. **Right Intention (Sammā-saṅkappa)** – Cultivating thoughts of goodwill, and harmlessness, avoiding harmful desires and ill-will.

Ethical Conduct (Śīla / Sīla)
3. **Right Speech (Sammā-vācā)** – Speaking truthfully, kindly, and avoiding lying, gossip, or harmful words

4. **Right Action (Sammā-kammanta)** – Acting ethically by resisting from harming living beings, stealing, and engaging in improper sexual conduct.

5. **Right Livelihood (Sammā-ājīva)** – Earning a living in a way that does not cause harm or exploit others.

Mental Discipline (Samādhi)
6. **Right Effort (Sammā-vāyāma)** – Cultivating positive states of mind, preventing negative thoughts, and striving for self-improvement.

7. **Right Mindfulness (Sammā-sati)** – Maintaining awareness of one's body, feelings, thoughts, and phenomena through consistent mindfulness practice.

8. **Right Concentration (Sammā-samādhi)** – Developing deep meditative states of focus to achieve insight and tranquility.

Like the Eightfold Path, The Eight Keys of Wisdom is a core teaching in ancient wisdom, drawing from Taoism, Buddhism, and Confucianism. It guides ethical conduct, mental discipline, and wisdom, leading to the cessation of suffering and enlightenment (*nirvana*).

Eight Keys of Wisdom
1. **Reflection** – See yourself as others see you

2. **Make correct choices** (Hun & Po) – Discerning true, right, and correct. Dealing with the inner conflict

3. **Overcome your delusion** – 5 agents, 7 distractions

4. **Turn on your light** – See and be seen, plant good seeds

5. **Be the mountain** – Attain honor rooted in principle

6. **Change your reality** – Assume responsibility of your fate or destiny

7. **Become a vessel of wisdom** – Practice what you preach, become a role model rather than a warning

8. **Water over fire** – Draw from nature's energies

Correlations Between the Eightfold Path and 8 Keys of Wisdom
1. **Reflection – Right View (Sammā-diṭṭhi)**

    o **Taoist Wisdom:** See yourself as others see you.

    o **Buddhist Parallel:** The Right View teaches seeing reality as it is, free from illusion. In Buddhism, self-awareness includes understanding how others perceive us and recognizing our attachments and biases.

2. **True, Right and Correct (Hun & Po) – Right Intention (Sammā-saṅkappa)**

    - **Taoist Wisdom:** Manage and cope with inner conflicts.
    - **Buddhist Parallel:** Right Intention involves aligning thoughts with ethical and wholesome goals, reducing inner conflict between desire (Po) and higher wisdom (Hun). Both traditions emphasize balancing these opposing aspects of the psyche.

3. **Overcome Your Delusion – Right Effort (Sammā-vāyāma)**

    - **Taoist Wisdom:** 5 agents, 7 distractions (Five Elements & Emotional Imbalances).
    - **Buddhist Parallel:** Right Effort means actively working to remove unwholesome states (such as greed, anger, and delusion) and cultivate wisdom. In Taoism, recognizing the interplay of the Five Elements and overcoming distractions aligns with maintaining mental clarity.

4. **Turn on Your Light – Right Mindfulness (Sammā-sati)**

    - **Taoist Wisdom:** See and be seen. Plant good seeds to leave a legacy of knowledge.
    - **Buddhist Parallel:** Right Mindfulness is about clear awareness of one's actions, emotions, and thoughts. "Turning on the light" in Taoism refers to conscious self-awareness, which aligns with the Buddhist practice of mindfulness meditation.

5. **Be the Mountain – Right Action (Sammā-kammanta)**

    - **Taoist Wisdom:** Achieve honor and respect by being rooted in principle.
    - **Buddhist Parallel:** Right Action means living with integrity, abstaining from harm and unethical behavior. Being "the mountain" represents stability in virtue, just as Right Action is about unwavering moral conduct.

6. **Change Your Reality – Right Livelihood (Sammā-ājīva)**

    - **Taoist Wisdom:** Assume responsibility for your fate or destiny.
    - **Buddhist Parallel:** Right Livelihood encourages earning a living ethically and shaping one's future through right choices. Taoism's view that we shape our destiny aligns with Buddhism's emphasis on karma and responsibility for one's path.

7. **Become the Vessel of Wisdom – Right Speech (Sammā-vācā)**

    - **Taoist Wisdom:** Practice what you preach. Strive to live as an example and not a warning to others.

- **Buddhist Parallel:** Right Speech teaches honest, compassionate communication. In Taoism, becoming a "vessel of wisdom" means embodying truth, much like Right Speech requires sincerity in words.

8. **Water Over Fire – Right Concentration (Sammā-samādhi)**
   - **Taoist Wisdom:** Balance the elements; maintain peace in chaos.
   - **Buddhist Parallel:** Right Concentration cultivates mental stillness and deep meditative absorption, similar to Taoist teachings on harmonizing the forces of water (yin) and fire (yang) to maintain balance and clarity.

Buddhist Eightfold Path	Taoist Eight Keys of Wisdom	Core Similarity
Right View (Sammā-diṭṭhi)	Reflection – See yourself as others see you	Self-awareness & perceiving reality as it is
Right Intention (Sammā-saṅkappa)	Po & Hun – Deal with the inner conflict	Aligning thoughts with wisdom and balance
Right Effort (Sammā-vāyāma)	Overcome Your Delusion – 5 agents, 7 distractions	Removing distractions & cultivating clarity
Right Mindfulness (Sammā-sati)	Turn on Your Light – See and be seen	Awareness of self and surroundings
Right Action (Sammā-kammanta)	Be the Mountain – Rooted in principle	Stability in moral conduct
Right Livelihood (Sammā-ājīva)	Change Your Reality – Assume responsibility for your destiny	Ethical living & shaping one's future
Right Speech (Sammā-vācā)	Become the Vessel of Wisdom – Practice what you preach	Integrity in words & actions
Right Concentration (Sammā-samādhi)	Water Over Fire – Balance the elements	Mental stillness & harmonizing opposites

The 8-Step Path to Achieve the Best Version of You

www.MindAndBodyExercises.com

A long-understood method of achieving harmony between one's mind, body and spirit, is this 8-Step Path. It has its origin in the ancient Chinese philosophy of Daoism but is highly relative to modern culture. The figure "8" is important to understand that as the infinity circle, there is no beginning nor end to entering into this process. It is a journey of self-awareness that can be entered into at any point throughout one's lifetime. Life is a challenge, and so is staying on this path of self-improvement. The reward is at the end of one's journey, knowing that they have pursued a meaningful life with direction and purpose.

1. Learning to Know Your "True Self"

By seeing & understanding your nature, self-reflection opens the door to the other steps of this process.

2. Making Correct Daily Choices

True / Right ← → Correct

Awareness of an inner "Moral Compass" to balance decisions by understanding true, right & correct.

3. Overcome Delusion of Your Thoughts & Ideas

You are not your thoughts. As consciousness you control your thoughts. Try not to be swayed by the mundane & trivial. Be solid like the root & not flippant like the leaves.

4. Cultivate Good Seeds to Pass On

Realize that you have a higher purpose beyond gaining material wealth and status. Be the light at the end of the tunnel.

5. Attain Honor

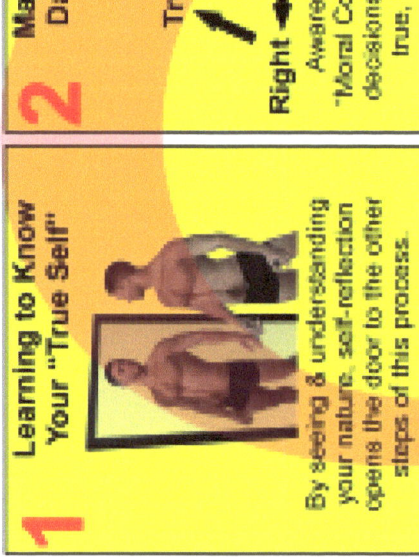

Live by principle - stand firm in what you believe, while allowing challenges to flow around you. Stand like a mountain, flow like a river.

6. Change Your Reality

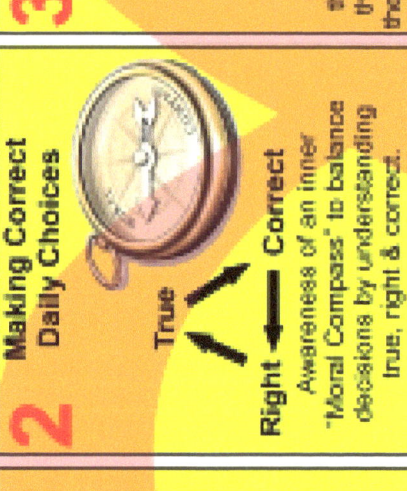

Understand that you are in control of your life and the choices you make determine your success or failure within your reality.

7. Become a Living Vessel of Wisdom

Knowledge alone is not power. The sharing of our knowledge is when knowledge becomes powerful.

8. Draw on Nature's Power

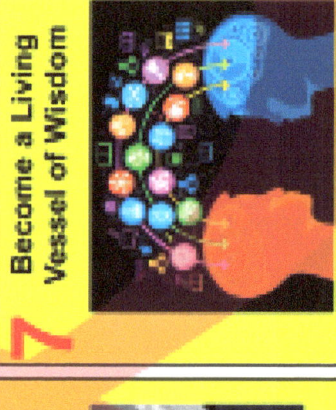

Qigong · Tai Chi · Baguazhang

Cultivate a strong mind, body & spirit by connecting to nature's fire, water & wind with sitting, standing & moving exercises.

c. Copyright 2018 - C4D Graphics Inc.

Wind and Water, Makes Fire

The human mind and body are integral parts of nature, constantly interacting with its energies. There is a direct correlation between the systems of nature and those of the body, with three key elements of wind, fire, and water, serving as points of connection.

- **Wind** corresponds to the respiratory system, as the air we breathe sustains life.

- **Fire** represents body temperature, which plays a vital role in all physiological functions.

- **Water** relates to the circulatory system, essential for vitality and well-being.

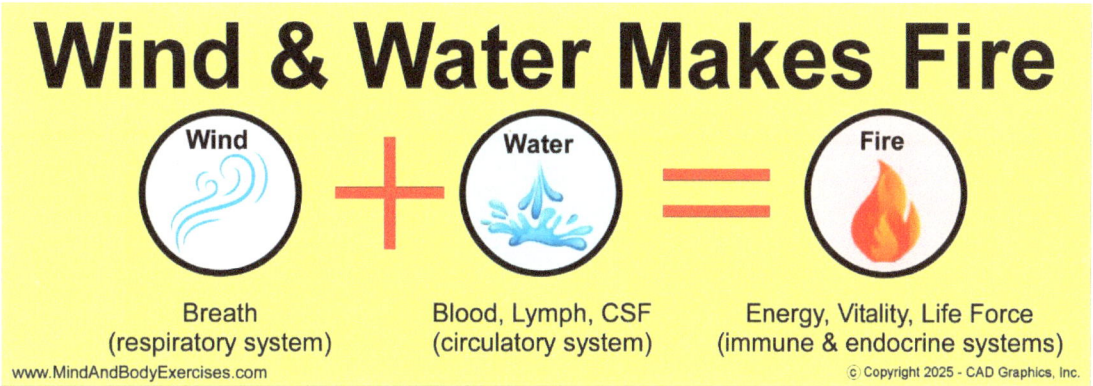

Practices such as Tai Chi, Qigong, and Bagua Zhang profoundly influence the body, impacting the organs, joints, and muscles at a deep level. In Taoist alchemy, the philosophical phrase *"wind and water make fire"* metaphorically represents the dynamic interactions of the Five Elements (Wu Xing) and the internal processes of self-cultivation.

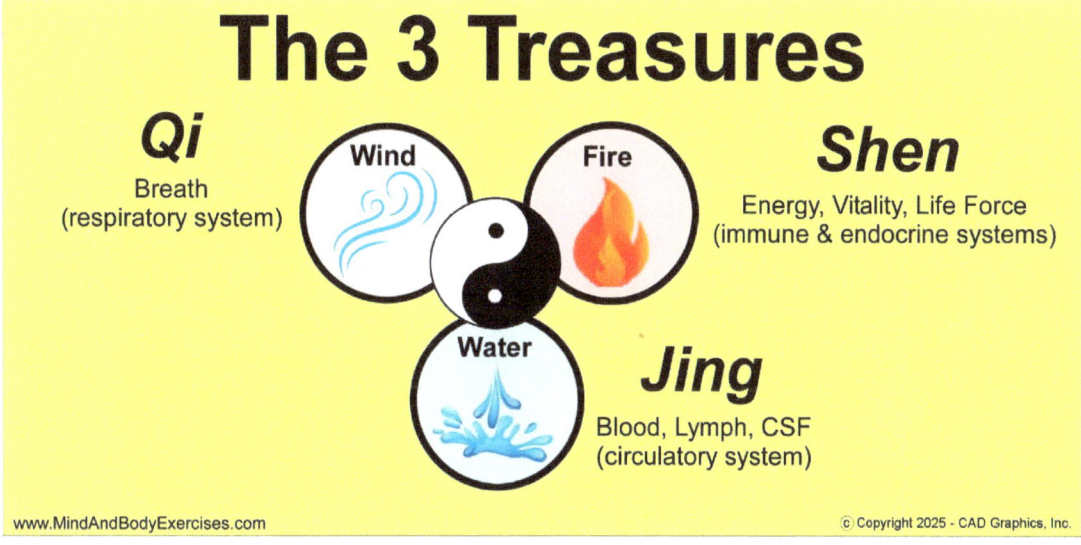

Here's a breakdown of how this concept fits into Taoist thought:

Five Elements Correspondence:

- **Wind (Feng, 风)** is often associated with Wood (Mu, 木), which represents growth, movement, and expansion.

- **Water (Shui, 水)** corresponds to the Kidneys and the essence (Jing), which serves as the foundation for transformation.

- **Fire (Huo, 火)** corresponds to Yang energy, warmth, and spirit (Shen).

- The idea is that the interaction of movement (Wind/Wood) and nourishment (Water) can generate Fire (Yang energy, transformation).

Neidan (Internal Alchemy) Interpretation:

- Wind (Wood) and Water represent Qi and Jing, respectively.

- Their controlled interaction through breathwork, meditation, and energy circulation can generate the internal ***"alchemy fire"*** needed to refine essence into Qi and Qi into Shen.

- This fire is not literal but the internal warmth and energetic transformation that happens in deep meditation or Qigong.

Martial & Qigong Perspective:

- In advanced Qigong and martial arts, regulated breath (Wind) and internal fluid movement (Water) manifest into internal heat (Fire), leading to refined power and vitality.

- This aligns with practices of Tai Chi, Qigong and BaguaZhang, where breath, body movement, and mind-intent cultivate the internal fire for vitality and martial efficiency.

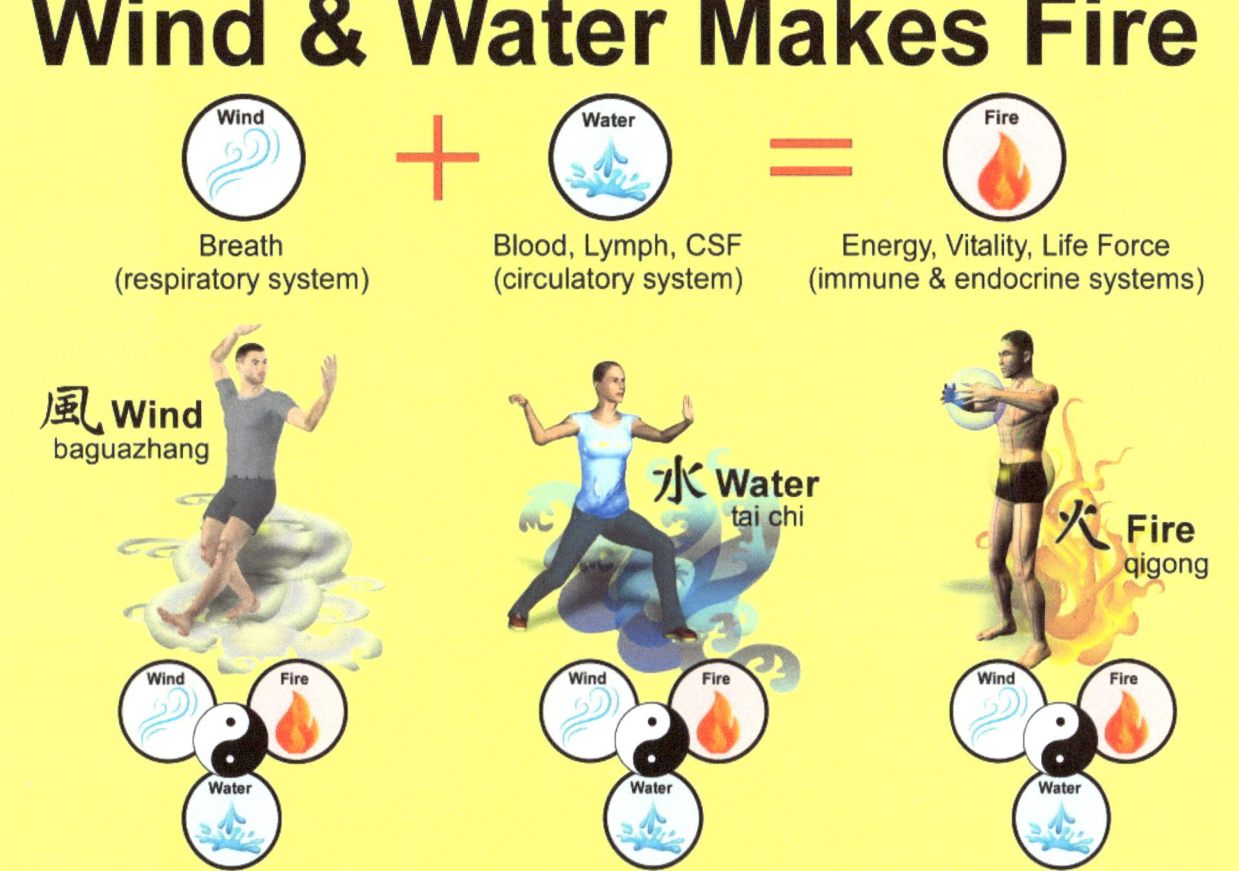

Gong De Wei Shen

The term **Gong De Wei Shen** (功德为神) could loosely be interpreted as "acquiring karmic merit for spiritual elevation or connection to the divine." It's a phrase that might not appear in ancient texts directly but captures the concept of dedicating good deeds or spiritual work to elevate one's spiritual state, aligning with Chinese philosophies of moral virtue influencing one's spiritual development. **Gong De Wei Shen** is indeed rooted in Chinese philosophical and spiritual traditions, though the exact expression isn't commonly cited. I will break it down to the best of my understanding:

1. **Gong (功):** This translates to merit, achievement, accomplishment, or work.

2. **Gong de (功德):** This translates to "merit" or "karmic merit" or virtuous deeds as used in Buddhist and Taoist traditions in the sense of virtue accumulated through good deeds and moral actions of generosity and compassion towards others. In traditional Chinese thought and in Buddhism, *gong de* is the spiritual merit or positive karma gained through altruistic actions, spiritual practice, and moral conduct. These merits are believed to contribute to spiritual growth and favorable outcomes in this life or future lives

3. **Wei (为):** This can mean "for" or "as" in this context, often used to imply that the merit serves or benefits something.

4. **Shen 神 :** This translates to "spirit" or "divine" and can suggest a higher spiritual state or connection with the divine.

While *gong de wei shen*, itself isn't a phrase widely cited in ancient texts, some numerous classical works and studies delve into the related concepts of *gong de* (karmic merit), the role of *shen* (spirit or divine), and the accumulation of spiritual merit through virtuous actions. Here are some references that explore these themes:

1. **Dao De Jing (Tao Te Ching)** by Lao Tzui: One of the foundational texts of Daoism, the *Dao De Jing* discusses concepts of virtue (*de*, 德) and alignment with the *Dao* (道) as a path to spiritual harmony. While it may not explicitly use *gong de*, it emphasizes the moral conduct and inner qualities that create harmony with the universe.

2. **The Avatamsaka Sutra (Huayan Sutra)**: In Mahayana Buddhism, which has heavily influenced Chinese thought, the *Avatamsaka Sutra* (华严经, *Huayan Jing*) explores the concept of *merit* (功德, *gong de*) in spiritual practice and its effect on one's path toward enlightenment. This text connects good deeds and moral actions with spiritual progression.

3. **The Book of Changes (I Ching)**: Though more symbolic, the *I Ching* reflects on the harmony between human actions and spiritual forces, suggesting that righteous behavior impacts one's fate and connection with higher powers.

4. **Zhuangzi**: This Daoist text, attributed to the philosopher Zhuang Zhou, explores spiritual transformation and the concept of *shen* as something cultivated through inner clarity and virtue.

The concepts of 功德 **(gong de, karmic merit)** and 神修 **(shen xiu, spiritual cultivation)** are deeply relevant to everyday life, even for those who don't actively follow Taoist or Buddhist traditions. Here's why they can be important:

1. Actions Shape Our Lives and Mindset

Every small act of kindness, generosity, or ethical behavior accumulates *gong de* not just in a spiritual sense but in how it influences your relationships, reputation, and self-perception. Helping a friend, being honest in business, or treating people with respect builds trust and goodwill, which can often return in unexpected ways.

2. Inner Peace Comes from Spiritual Awareness

Spiritual cultivation (*shen xiu*) isn't about being religious, but rather developing self-awareness, clarity, and emotional balance. In daily life, this may be practiced as:
- Pausing before reacting negatively in a stressful situation.
- Practicing mindfulness or gratitude to reduce anxiety.
- Seeking wisdom in challenges rather than reacting impulsively.

3. Good Energy Attracts Good Outcomes

Many people unconsciously follow the idea of karma or energetic reciprocity. When you consistently act with integrity and positive intention, life tends to reflect that back. We sometimes call this *"what goes around, comes around."* This is why some who choose to cultivate *gong de* often experience more fulfilling relationships, career success, and personal growth.

4. Resilience in Hard Times

Practicing *gong de* and *shen xiu* helps you build inner strength. When facing setbacks, those who have cultivated patience, kindness, and wisdom may be better equipped to manage challenges with grace, rather than feeling like a victim of circumstances.

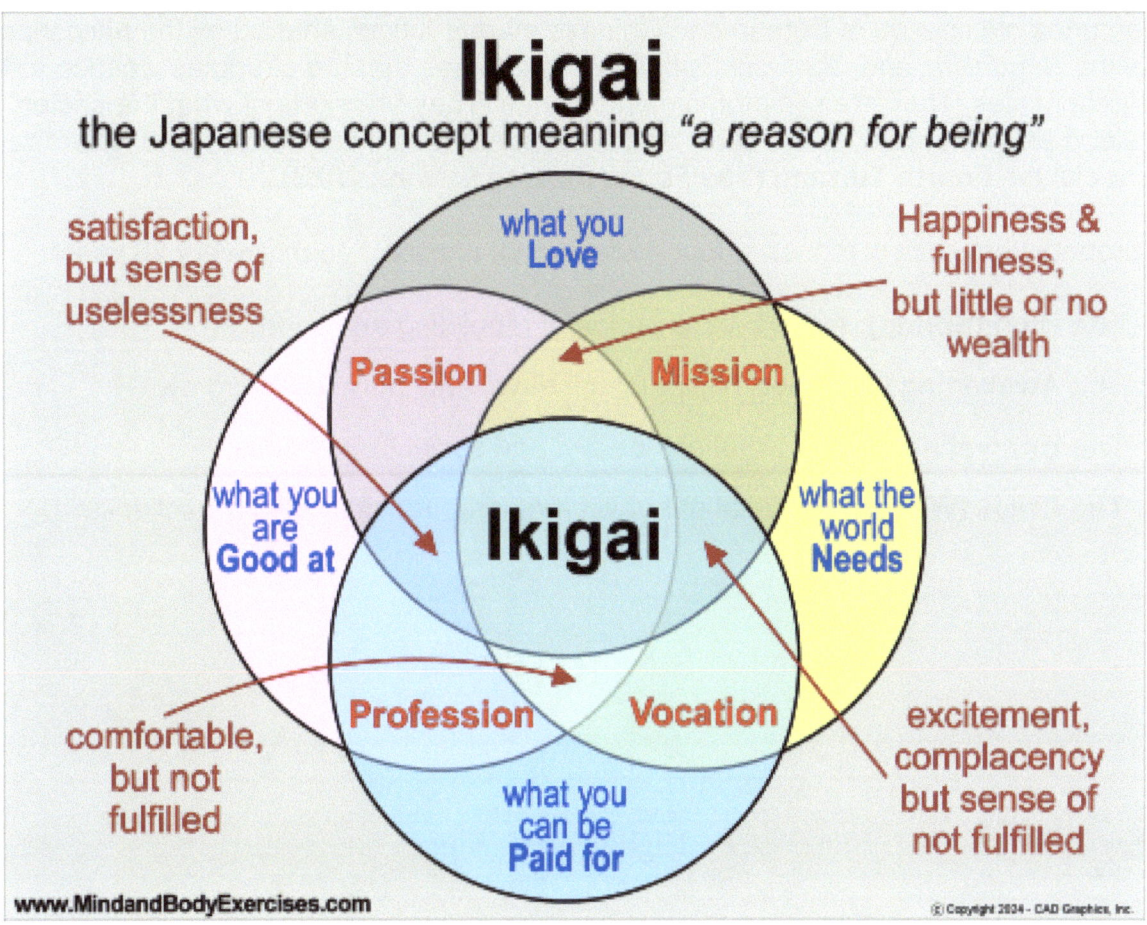

5. A Sense of Purpose

Beyond material success, many people seek meaning in their daily lives. The Japanese term of **Ikigai** embodies the concept of meaning, purpose along with other aspects of passion and profession.. Spiritual cultivation (*shen xiu*) can provide a sense of meaning or purpose, whether through meditation, learning, creative expression, or simply striving to be a better person.

In Summary

These aren't just ancient ideas, but rather practical tools for striving to live a more peaceful, balanced, and fulfilling life. By cultivating merit (*gong de*) and refining your inner spirit (*shen xiu*), one may naturally create a more harmonious life, both for themselves and those around them.

The Warrior, the Scholar, and the Sage

A Daoist View of Strength, Decline, and Human Destiny

In every era, civilizations rise and fall, not by accident or coincidence, but by the rhythm of deeper patterns or cycles of virtue and decay, clarity and confusion. As someone connected to a centuries-old lineage of Korean and Chinese martial artists, shaped by the philosophies of *Taoism, Buddhism*, and *Confucianism*, I've come to see that the struggles we face today are not anomalies. They are symptoms of imbalance. They are signs of what the ancients understood as the *"return to the Dao"* and what modern thinkers Strauss and Howe have come to call the **Fourth Turning** (*The Fourth Turning Is Here*, 2023).

They propose that society moves in four generational phases, roughly every 20 years:

- **The High (Spring):** After crisis, a period of rebuilding and cohesion.
- **The Awakening (Summer):** Spiritual upheaval and individualism grow.
- **The Unraveling (Fall):** Institutions decay, and social trust erodes.
- **The Crisis (Winter):** A pivotal upheaval requiring transformation or collapse.

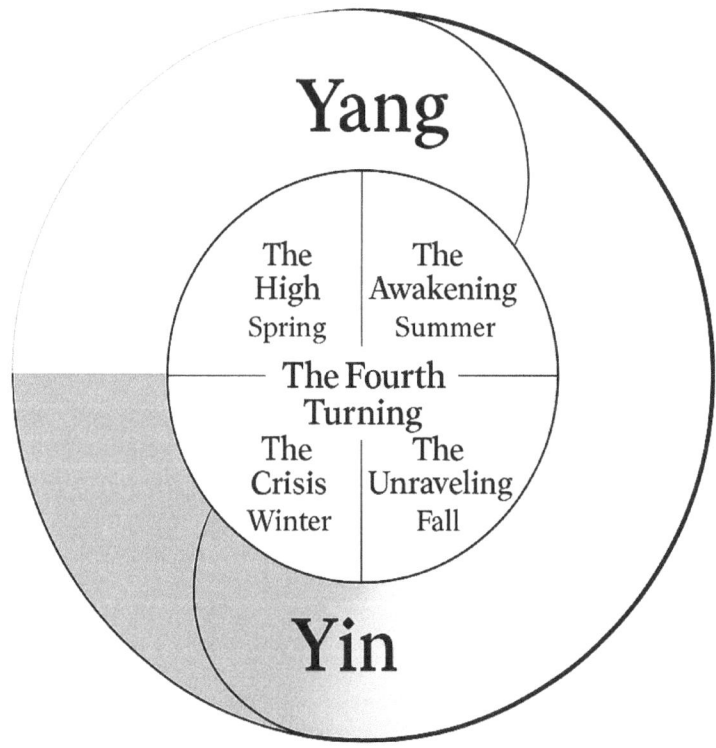

We have witnessed this over many years of history, such as the Fourth Turning (crisis) of the Great Depression into World War II, followed by a post-WWII boom in the U.S. (the High), then the 1960s counterculture movement (the Awakening), followed by the 1980s-2000s in the U.S. (Unraveling) and now into another 20 years of crisis. According to this model, we are now in the Fourth Turning or the winter phase, marked by turbulence, institutional failure, and a call for redefinition. Taoism would simply say: *the yang must return.* The old forms have decayed; the new must be forged through effort and alignment with the Dao.

At the heart of this worldview is the triad of ***jing (essence), qi (energy)***, and ***shen* (spirit)**. These internal forces are not just concepts from Taoist cultivation; they represent three powerful human archetypes:

- **The Warrior (Jing)** - grounded in physical vitality, courage, and action.
- **The Scholar (Qi)** - representing knowledge, refinement, and discernment.
- **The Sage (Shen)** - embodying spiritual clarity, stillness, and alignment with the eternal.

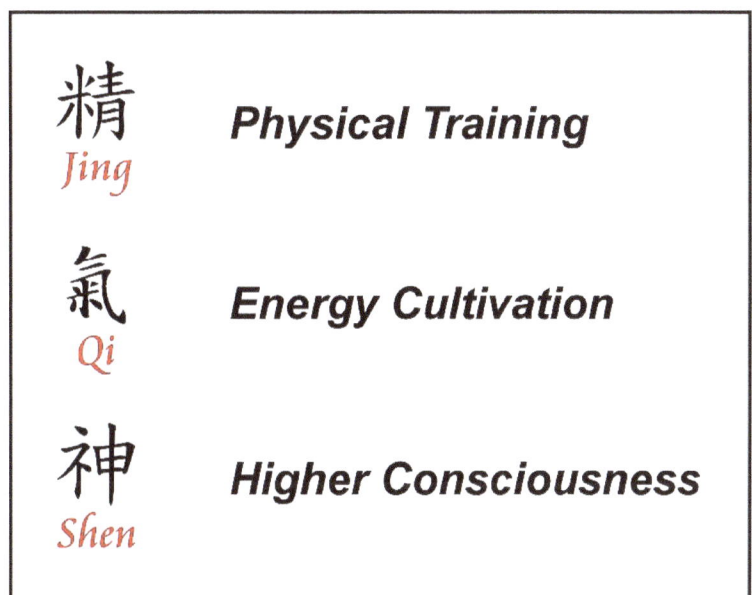

This trinity mirrors the natural progression of human development and when lived out collectively, forms the foundation of a resilient, ethical, and awakened society. The warrior, the scholar, and the sage can be found in various walks of life.

The Cycles of Strength and Decline

You've likely heard the saying:
> *"Hard times create strong men,*
> *strong men create good times,*
> *good times create weak men,*
> *and weak men create hard times."*

This isn't just a catchy aphorism, but a succinct summary of **yin** and **yang**, the core principle of Taoist cosmology. When yang (strength, discipline, clarity) reaches its peak, it gives way to yin (softness, comfort, passivity). When yin becomes excessive, yang reasserts itself through challenge, hardship, and the need for resilience.

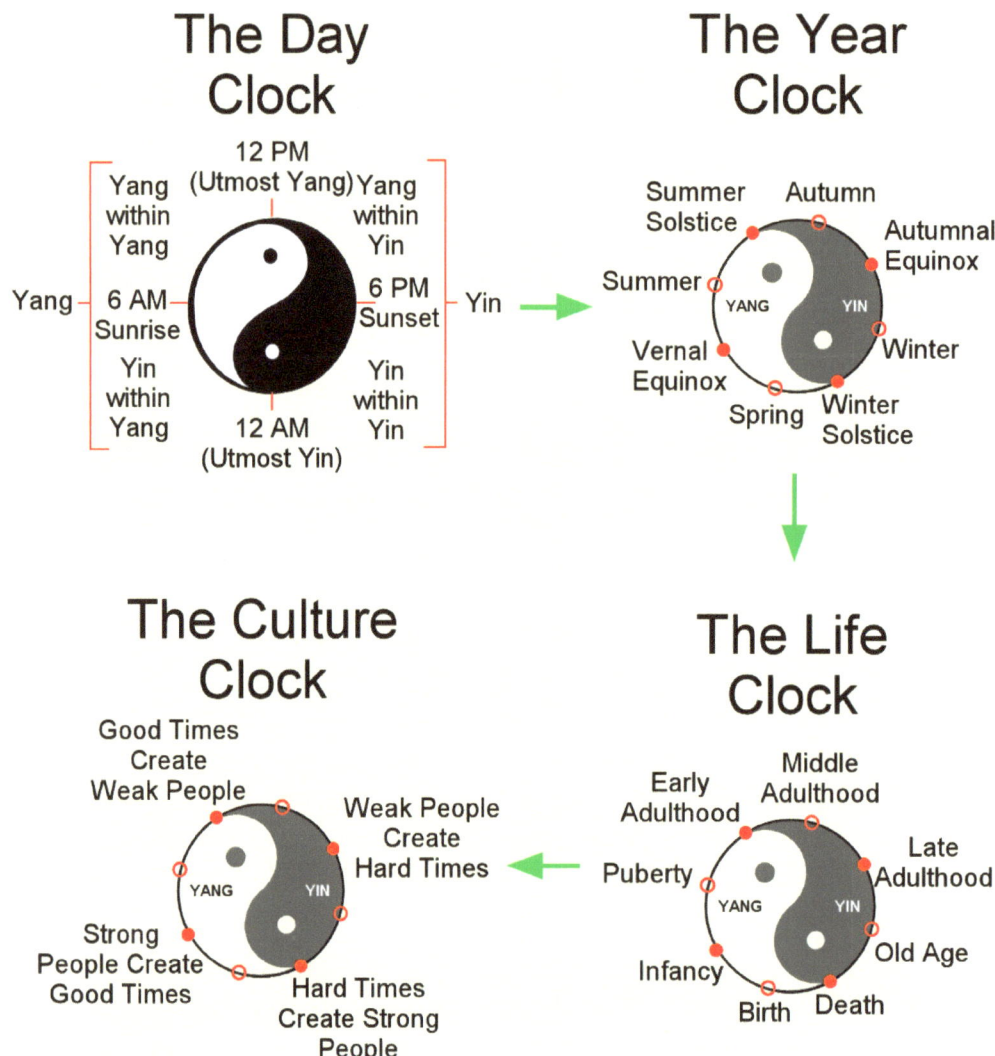

When Good Men Do Nothing

The phrase:

> "The only thing necessary for the triumph of evil is for good men to do nothing,"

It resonates even more powerfully during times like these.

In the comfort of past decades, the "good times" many laid down the tools of vigilance. Warriors stopped training. Scholars stopped questioning. Sages retreated into the background. This absence of cultivated moral men (and I emphasize cultivated, not simply physically strong or formally educated) created a vacuum where mediocrity, passivity, and manipulation took root.

The Dao doesn't punish. It corrects. The correction is not emotional but rather structural, rhythmic, and natural. In a time of unraveling, those who choose to do nothing only deepen the descent. Those who act in alignment with virtue help midwife the rebirth.

Cultivation Is the Cure

In our tradition, we don't look outward to blame, but rather we look inward to refine ourselves through:

- Cultivating **jing** through martial discipline and physical integrity.
- Building **qi** through breathwork, mindfulness, and mental refinement.
- Elevating **shen** through spiritual practice, service, and contemplation.

This process isn't merely for personal benefit, but hopefully to provide a model for society. In this Fourth Turning, we need a return of those who live as warriors of integrity, scholars of discernment, and Sages of wisdom. Their presence creates coherence in chaos. The Dao teaches that when the inner is aligned, the outer begins to harmonize.

The Role of Men in the Turning

Throughout history, men have often occupied positions of leadership, warfare, and infrastructure in roles requiring strength, vision, and responsibility. When these roles are filled by individuals of weak moral character, or by those disconnected from the natural order of the Dao, decline does not merely begin but it accelerates.

In today's world, we're witnessing the fallout of this imbalance. *Divine masculinity* is rooted in strength, service, wisdom, and responsibility has been overshadowed by its distorted reflection or *toxic masculinity,* which is driven by ego, control, irresponsibility, and impulse. The difference between the two is not force, but character.

The danger does not lie in masculinity itself, but in its misdirection. When yang energy is active, outward, and forceful it becomes unmoored from purpose and virtue, it devolves into recklessness, violence, and domination. One doesn't have to look far to see the consequences: our prisons are full, crime persists, and too many men choose instant gratification over disciplined action.

Morally weak men are the most dangerous to society. Not because of their gender, but because of their inability to withstand temptation, make principled choices, or lead by example. Without the internal refinement of jing, qi, and shen, there is no foundation for restraint or wisdom.

Yet in the same breath, we must acknowledge that society still deeply depends on strong men in body, mind, and spirit. It is men who fight in wars, build bridges, maintain power grids,

work oil rigs, harvest timber, and risk their lives in roles essential to our survival and stability. These are not outdated relics of a bygone age. They are the backbone of civilization.
But physical strength alone is not enough. In a time like the Fourth Turning, we don't just need capable men. We need **cultivated men**:

- Men who have mastered their emotions and instincts.
- Men who serve rather than dominate.
- Men who fight when necessary but protect by nature.
- Men who think, reflect, and align with something greater than themselves.

As the Dao teaches:

Softness without structure leads to collapse. Force without wisdom leads to tyranny.

The cure is not to suppress masculine energy but to elevate it, refine it, and align it with the eternal flow of the Dao.

In this age of unraveling, the world doesn't need less masculinity. It needs truer masculinity. The kind forged in hardship, guided by virtue, and embodied by the **Warrior, the Scholar, and the Sage**.

Conclusion: Dao and the Fourth Turning

If everything follows the Dao, then this present upheaval is not a mistake. It's a call.
A call to remember. To return. To rebuild.

The Fourth Turning is not a death sentence. It is an initiation. Just as in Taoist cultivation, decay gives way to rebirth. The yang returns only when yin has gone to its extreme.
We must ask ourselves:

- Will we wait for others to restore balance?
- Or will we embody the Warrior, the Scholar, and the Sage, and rise to meet the moment?

The Dao is not just a path. It is the pattern of life itself. To walk it now, consciously is to become part of the cure.

Reference:

The fourth turning is here. (2023, July 18). Book by Neil Howe | Official Publisher Page | Simon & Schuster. https://www.simonandschuster.com/books/The-Fourth-Turning-Is-Here/Neil-Howe/9781982173739

Be the Warrior, the Scholar, the Sage - a Blueprint to Happiness & Purpose

Jing (Essence)

Warrior Phase

Through practicing physical movements (Jing - essence), one can better develop:

1) Awareness – realization, perception or knowledge

2) Memory – the process of reproducing or recalling what has been learned or experienced

3) Coordination – bring actions together into a smooth concerted way

4) Control – skill in the use of restraint, direction and coordination

5) Endurance – ability to tolerate stress or hardship

6) Strength – power to resist or exert force

7) Stamina – combination of endurance and strength

8) Speed – rate of motion

9) Power – might or influence

10) Reflex – end result of reception, transmission and reaction

11) Strategy – a careful plan or method to achieve a goal

Mentally, these character traits are nurtured & refined:

Respect

Discipline

Self Esteem

Confidence

Determination to Achieve Goals

Qi (Energy)

Scholar Phase

Through practicing mental exercises (Qigong - vitality), one can better develop:

1) Relaxation of the muscles

2) Building of internal power

3) Strengthening of the organs

4) Improving the cardiopulmonary function

5) Strengthening the nerves

6) Improving vascular function

7) Can be practiced by the seriously ill

8) Help prevent injury to joints, ligaments & bones

9) Quicken recovery time from injuries & surgery

10) Building of athletic & martial arts power

11) Lessening of stress & balances emotions

12) Benefits sedentary individuals

Mentally, these concepts are comprehended & assimilated:

Human anatomy & physiology

Energy flow (Qi) with the energy meridians

Structural alignment of the skeletal & muscular systems

Shen (Spirit)

Sage Phase

Through practicing mediation exercises (Shen - consciousness), one can develop better understanding of:

1) The origin, nature, and character of things and beings

2) The human condition - study of human nature and conditions of life

3) The importance of communication on many different levels in order to share and disseminate wisdom

4) Sense of purpose

5) Making a difference

6) Self-less service to others

7) The inter-relationship between one another and how that can determine cause and effect

8) Our interaction between humans and the world (universe) we exist in

www.MindandBodyExercises.com

© Copyright 2023 - CAD Graphics, Inc.

"Man Divides Heaven and Earth"

The concept of **"Man divides Heaven and Earth"** is a fundamental idea in Chinese philosophy, particularly in Daoism and Confucian thought. It relates to the idea that humanity serves as a bridge between **Heaven (天, Tiān)** and **Earth (地, Dì)**—two fundamental cosmic forces.

Key Aspects of the Concept:
1. **The Triad of Heaven, Earth, and Man**

    - Heaven represents the formless, the celestial, the spiritual, and the governing natural laws.
    - Earth represents the material, the manifested, the physical world, and stability.
    - Man is the mediator, possessing both spiritual (Heaven) and physical (Earth) aspects.
    - Humans impose order, create divisions, and establish structures to align with the Dao.

2. **Humanity as the Harmonizer**

    - Humans have the unique ability to observe natural rhythms (from Heaven) and adapt them to earthly existence.
    - Through philosophy, morality, and governance, humans bring order, such as dividing time into calendars, measuring space, and establishing social structures.

3. **Yin-Yang and Five Elements Influence**

    - This idea ties into yin-yang theory because man, in the middle, balances opposing forces.
    - It also aligns with the Five Elements (or Phases) (Wu Xing) since humans categorize and interact with nature based on these elemental relationships.

4. **Practical Applications**

    - In Confucianism, it applies to ethics, social roles, and proper conduct.
    - In Daoism, it relates to aligning human actions with the Dao and achieving balance.
    - In traditional Chinese medicine (TCM), it explains the body's role as a microcosm of the universe.

"Heaven and Earth, Turned Upside Down"

"Heaven and Earth, Turned Upside Down" is a phrase that means a complete and radical upheaval or change, signifying a situation where the established order is completely disrupted and everything is thrown into chaos as if the natural order of the universe has been reversed; essentially, a dramatic and significant change where the normal way of things is completely overturned.

The concept of "Heaven and Earth, turned upside down" appears in various Chinese philosophical and esoteric traditions, including Daoism (I Ching), and martial arts. It often symbolizes a reversal of natural order, transformation, or a shift in perception.

Possible Interpretations:

1. **Reversal of Cosmic Order**
    - Normally, Heaven (Yang) is above, and Earth (Yin) is below. Flipping this order suggests a paradox, disorder, or a fundamental transformation of reality.
    - It can imply chaos, breaking norms, or a cosmic shift that forces new perspectives.

2. **Daoist Alchemy & Inner Transformation**
    - In Daoist internal alchemy (Neidan), reversing Heaven and Earth can symbolize inner transformation, where the ordinary world is transcended.
    - It is sometimes associated with the *Microcosmic Orbit* practice, where energy (*Qi*) circulates against its usual flow to achieve spiritual enlightenment.

3. **I Ching Influence**
    - Certain hexagrams in the I Ching hint at the reversal of Heaven and Earth, representing a dramatic change, like Hexagram 12 (Pí, Stagnation) vs. Hexagram 11 (Tài, Peace).
    - When the natural order is disrupted, it can indicate a need for adaptation, renewal, or a deeper understanding of balance.

4. **Martial Arts & Strategy**
    - Some martial philosophies refer to this idea in unexpected tactics, adaptability, and overturning conventional wisdom in combat.
    - It relates to Sun Tzu's "Art of War" principles, where flipping the expected order creates strategic advantage.

5. **Spiritual Awakening & Perception Shift**
    - A mystical interpretation suggests seeing beyond illusion *(Maya)* or breaking free from conventional thought.
    - It resonates with Zen and Chan Buddhism's use of paradox to awaken deeper understanding.

"Born With Nothing, Die With Nothing"

The concept of **"born with nothing, die with nothing"** is a profound philosophical idea found in many Eastern traditions, including Buddhism and Taoism. It reflects the principles of impermanence, detachment, and the cyclical nature of existence. We enter this world with no possessions, and when we leave, we take nothing with us. This underscores the transient nature of material wealth and highlights the deeper value of experiences, relationships, and inner growth.

Happiness is not about collecting material things or beautiful memories. It is about having a deep feeling of contentment and knowing that life is a blessing. – Jeigh Ilano

This idea extends beyond human life to all living beings, aligning with the concept of "no beginning, no end." Like the yin-yang (☯) and infinity (∞) symbols, it represents the continuous flow of transformation, where emptiness gives rise to form, and form dissolves back into emptiness.

"Born with nothing, die with nothing" reflects the cyclical nature of existence not just humans but all living organisms, aligning with the concept of "no beginning, no end." Like the yin-yang and infinity symbols, it represents the continuous flow of transformation where emptiness gives rise to form, and form dissolving back into emptiness.

Human life can be seen as consciousness temporarily residing in form, experiencing the ever-shifting balance of existence before returning to the formless. In Taoism, this mirrors the **Dao** (道), the ever-flowing source from which all things arise and to which they ultimately return. Just as yin transforms into yang and vice versa, life and death are not endpoints but expressions of an eternal process. This perspective encourages non-attachment, balance, and harmony with the natural flow of life, recognizing that all physical possessions are ultimately borrowed, and everything returns to the Dao.

Related Concepts:

Biblical Perspective: A similar idea appears in the Book of Job, where Job states, "The Lord gave, and the Lord has taken away; may the name of the Lord be praised." This is often interpreted as an acceptance of life's impermanence, acknowledging that all we have is ultimately a gift and can be withdrawn at any time.

The Heart Sutra: A central text in Mahayana Buddhism, the Heart Sutra articulates the nature of emptiness, stating that all phenomena bear the mark of emptiness—their true nature is beyond birth and death, being and non-being.

Śūnyatā (Emptiness): In Mahayana Buddhism, śūnyatā refers to the understanding that all things are devoid of intrinsic existence. This insight is fundamental to recognizing the transient nature of life and the absence of a permanent self.

Samsara: This term describes the continuous cycle of birth, death, and rebirth, emphasizing the impermanence and suffering inherent in worldly existence.

Why This Concept Matters in Everyday Life

Understanding and embracing this concept can have a profound impact on how we approach daily life. It reminds us to focus on what truly matters. Our experiences, relationships, and inner development are most important, rather than being overly attached to material possessions or fleeting successes. By recognizing the impermanent nature of all things, we can cultivate greater resilience and gratitude in the face of challenges, reduce unnecessary stress, and live with greater appreciation and mindfulness.

This perspective encourages us to be present in each moment, to value the people around us, and to engage in life with a sense of peace and acceptance. It also promotes generosity and compassion, as we recognize that nothing truly belongs to us, and what we give to others is ultimately part of the greater flow of all existence.

By implementing this understanding into our lives, we can develop a deeper sense of harmony, balance, and contentment, freeing ourselves from the burdens of attachment and fear while embracing the natural rhythms of life.

C: Moral Psychology, Truth & Perception

Philosophy or Religion?

Buddhism, Taoism, and Confucianism – a comparison of the 3 systems

There is often debate as to what a philosophy is, versus that which is a religion. I have come to understand that there are fundamental differences between the two that are rooted in the goals, nature, and methods of each system. Religion seems to focus mostly on spiritual awareness through understanding and moral guidance, whereas philosophy embodies more broad topics such as science, logic, politics, and art. Philosophy looks to find truth in empirical and logical evidence, while religion usually accepts faith as valid evidence. Philosophy can be a broader, and more general field, where religion usually involves specific sets of beliefs and practices within a group. Philosophical aspects often appear within religions and consequently philosophical discussions about religious topics. The relationship between philosophy and religion can be complementary, where each can offer a unique perspective of human experience.

I write about this topic as I have found that individuals who have some type of relationship with either a life philosophy or religion, often have a stronger sense of purpose, meaning and gratitude beyond themselves. This often leads to a healthier and happier life. Also, association with a religion while aligning with a philosophical system need not be mutually exclusive to one another. In various parts of the world where people are free to worship and live as they may, one can be a Christian, Buddhist and Taoist if they so choose.

Buddhism, Taoism, and **Confucianism** are three of the most commonly practiced belief systems that are often labeled as philosophies, religions or even sometimes as both. The following is a summary of their origins and tenets:

The 8-spoked wheel is often seen as a symbol for Buddhism.

Buddhism:
Origin:
- Buddhism was founded in the 6th century BCE by Buddha (563-483 BCE), also named Siddhartha Gautama, in ancient India which is today Nepal.
- Siddhartha was a prince who gave up his privileged life in order to better understand the nature of human suffering and to seek enlightenment or *nirvana*.

Core Tenets:
- The Four Noble Truths define the nature of suffering and a path to reduce its presence:
    - The Truth of Suffering (*Dukkha*): Buddhism acknowledges the existence of suffering and dissatisfaction in life. This suffering can be physical, emotional, or mental.
    - The Truth of the Cause of Suffering (*Samudaya*): Buddhism asserts that the root cause of suffering is craving or attachment (tanha) to things that are impermanent. This attachment leads to suffering because everything in the world is subject to change and eventual loss.
    - The Truth of the Cessation of Suffering (*Nirodha*): Buddhism teaches that it is possible to end suffering by letting go of attachment and craving. When one ceases to cling to impermanent things, suffering can be extinguished.
    - The Truth of the Path to the Cessation of Suffering (*Magga*): Buddhism offers a practical path called the Eightfold Path that leads to the cessation of suffering. This path consists of ethical and mental practices, such as right understanding, right intention, right speech, right action, right livelihood, right effort, right mindfulness, and right concentration.

- The Eight-fold Path provides a guide towards ethical and mental development needed to achieve enlightenment (Nirvana):
    - Right views

- Right aspirations
- Right speech
- Right conduct
- Right livelihood
- Right endeavor
- Right mindfulness
- Right meditation

Goal:
- The ultimate goal in Buddhism is to attain Nirvana, where there is a state of liberation from the continuous cycle of birth, death, and rebirth also known as *Samsara.*

The *taijitsu* is often associated with Taoism and its concept of yin & yang.

Taoism:
Origin:
- Taoism, or sometimes *Daoism*, thought to have originated from Lao Tzu and his foundational text of the *Tao Te Ching* (The Way and Its Power), in China in the 6th century BCE.

Core Tenets:
- Main focus is upon trying to live in accordance to the *Tao* (the Way), which is thought to be the indefinable, fundamental force that unites all and everything in the universe.
- Another main principle is that of *Wu Wei* (effortless action), where one strives to live in harmony within the natural flow of the Tao rather than be subject to it.
- *Ying & yang* focuses upon the unity and duality inherent in all seeming opposites, such as: night-day, male-female, good-evil, positive-negative, etc.

Goal:
- Taoist philosophy strives to have the individual exist in a state of balance and harmony with the Tao, in order to align within the natural order of things, rather than imposing one's own will upon nature and the universe as a whole.

The Chinese character for water is often associated with Confucianism.

Confucianism:
Origin:
- Confucianism originated in China and was founded by Confucius (also known as Kong Fuzi) (551-479 BCE).
- Confucius was primarily concerned with understanding social order and its issues of ethics, morality, and the proper conduct of people living in society.

Core Tenets:
- Sacred texts of the *Wu Ching* (Five Classics) include the *I Ching* (Book of Changes), the *Lun-Yu* (The Analects)
- Emphasis is upon a moral code of:
    - *Li*: A code of moral/social conduct
    - *Jen*: Compassion/benevolence towards others
    - *Yi*: Righteousness
    - *Te*: Virtue
    - *Xiao*: Filial piety
- The importance of social harmony and the cultivation of moral character through education and self-cultivation.
- Emphasis upon the "Golden Rule" of "do not do unto others what you would not desire yourself."

Goal:
- Confucianism focuses upon establishing and maintaining a harmoniously functioning, well-ordered society through the virtuous persons who can fulfill their roles and responsibilities for the greater good of all.

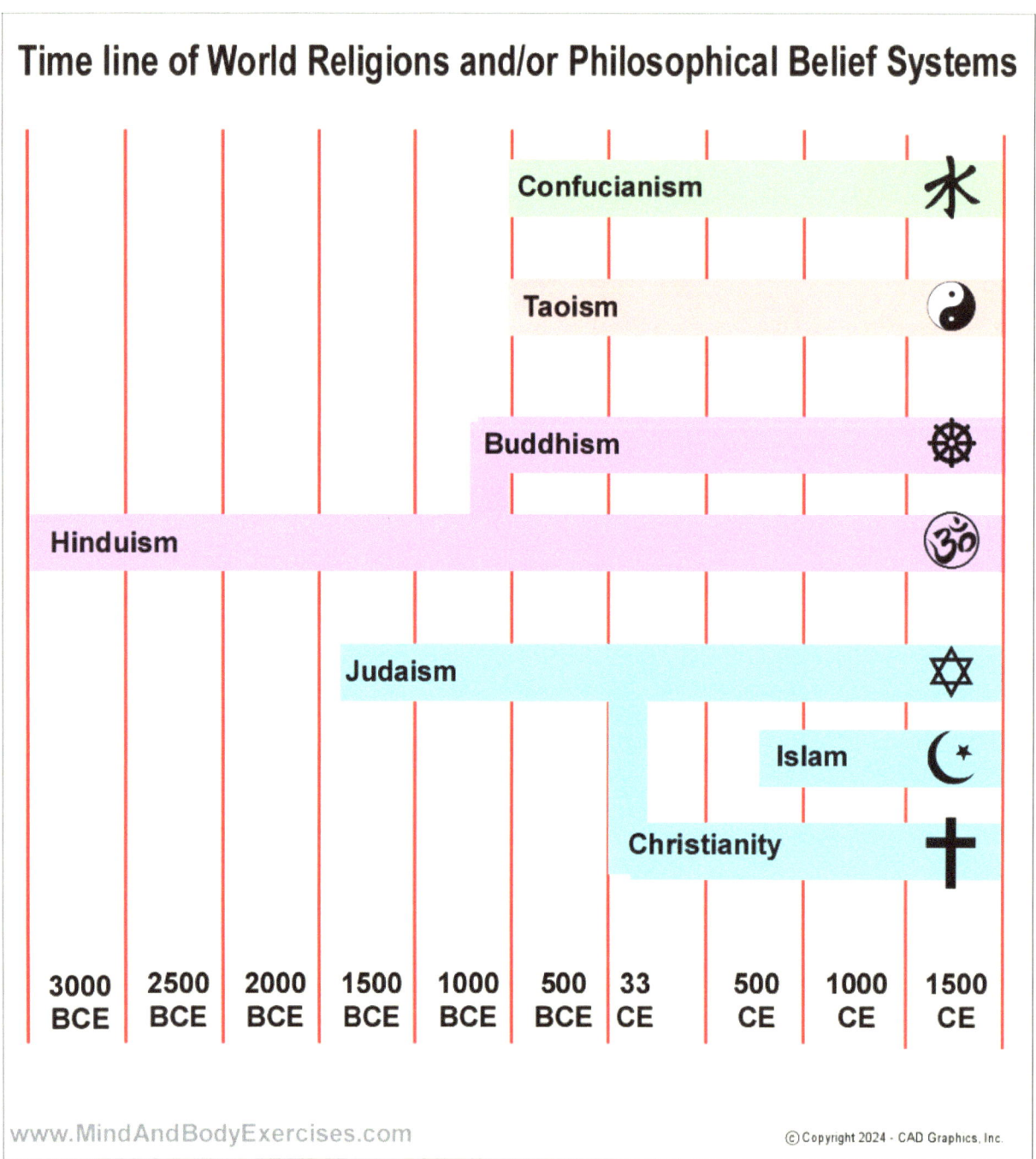

From my research, there is no historical evidence that supports that the founders of Buddhism (Siddhartha Gautama), Taoism (Lao Tzu), and Confucianism (Confucius) had ever met one another, crossed paths or had interactions during their lifetimes. All three of these individuals lived in different times and places. Based upon the geographical distances as well as cultural differences between them, it is quite unlikely that these founders could have shared any direct experience or even knowledge of each other's existence.

These traditions often share some of the same philosophical ideas. Similarities in philosophical topics cultivated by these systems are most likely due to common exploration of universal ethical and existential questions during their times, rather than direct interactions or encounters among the founders. These systems do also have unique differences in their goals, teachings, methods, traditions, and approaches to life.

Comparisons between the three systems:
- **Basic Goals:**
    - Buddhism: understanding the self.
    - Taoism: understanding the self in relation to all else.
    - Confucianism: understanding the self and the relationship to society.

- **Geographic Origins:**
    - Buddhism: India
    - Taoism: China
    - Confucianism: China

- **Founders:**
    - Buddhism: Siddhartha Gautama (Buddha)
    - Taoism: Often associated with Lao Tzu
    - Confucianism: Confucius

- **Central Concepts:**
    - Buddhism: Four Noble Truths, Eightfold Path, nirvana
    - Taoism: Tao, wu wei, yin & yang
    - Confucianism: Li, Jen, Te, Yi, Xiao

- **Ultimate Goal:**
    - Buddhism: Nirvana
    - Taoism: Harmony with the Tao
    - Confucianism: Social harmony through moral character and cultivation

- **Perspective on Life:**
    - Buddhism: reduce suffering, detach from desires.
    - Taoism: alignment and harmony with the Tao
    - Confucianism: ethical conduct and social responsibilities

True, Right, and Correct

I have engaged in quite a few discussions regarding "truth" with others over my years. I have learned from my observations and in particular that "kind words are seldom true; true words are seldom kind". True words can be uncomfortable or even painful for the speaker as well as the recipient. But like you stated, being a desirable dinner guest might not be your goal.

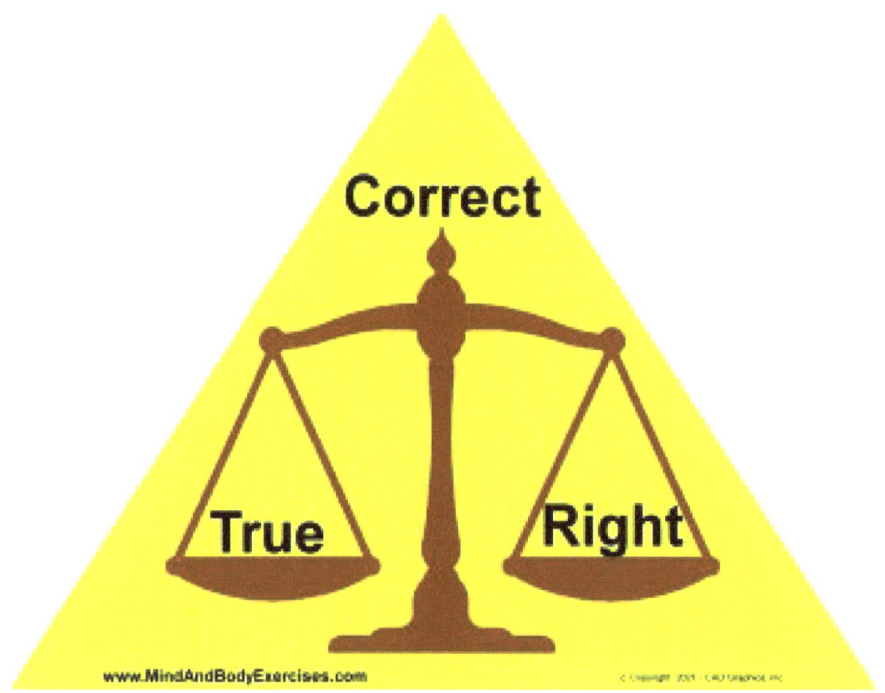

I was taught from my experiences within martial arts and its background in Taoism, Buddhism and Confucianism, the concept of balancing true, right and correct. We often find ourselves trying to balance ourselves between what is true, right or correct for any given situation and particular circumstances for any specific time and place. What was true yesterday may not be today. What is appropriate in one setting, may not be for another. If we tell the truth to a young child about birth, murder, drugs and other complex subjects, before their understanding is appropriate, it may cause damage to their perspectives for years to come. However, if we do what we feel is right and maybe shield them from reality, this too may cause potential issues down the road. Correct, however, is the balance we seek to find between true and right. So, in other words, I do not think the truth is totally absolute and appropriate for all situations.

Wisdom is a recipe of knowledge and experience obtained over time (age) allowing one to differentiate when the correct timing is to react or not to react. When to do, when not to do. Coming up to a stop sign, you really don't care to stop your vehicle (your true feeling) but you do because it is the right action (the law) to stop. If a blaring fire engine were to suddenly appear in your rear-view mirror, you might choose to move through the intersection and to a space clear of the oncoming 370,000 pounds of moving metal and water (correct action for this situation).

Beyond Critical Thinking: The True, Right, and Correct Framework

In an age dominated by speed, data, and polarization, the need for wise decision-making has never been greater. While traditional critical thinking focuses on logic and evidence, it often omits other dimensions of human understanding, such as authenticity, ethics, and contextual appropriateness. The "True, Right, and Correct" framework expands critical thinking into a multidimensional model that integrates intellectual rigor with moral clarity and practical wisdom.

This model draws from philosophical reasoning, spiritual awareness, and functional discernment to offer a more holistic approach to evaluating choices, actions, and beliefs.

Expanding Critical Thinking: A Holistic Triad

Critical thinking is often defined as the ability to analyze, evaluate, and synthesize information in order to form reasoned judgments. It relies on logic, evidence, skepticism, and reasoning. However, while these tools are necessary, they are not always sufficient.

The "True, Right, and Correct" framework offers a layered upgrade to conventional critical thinking:

Aspect	Conventional Critical Thinking	True-Right-Correct Framework
Logic	Essential	Integrated within "Right"
Ethics	Optional or minimal	Central under "True"
Authenticity	Rarely addressed	Essential under "True"
Intuition/Conscience	Often ignored	Embraced within "True" and "Right"
Functional Aptness	Sometimes included	Core under "Correct"

Overview of the Two-lens Model

The framework is visualized as a Venn diagram with two intersecting circles and the portion that overlaps to form a third zone:

- **TRUE** – Inner authenticity and alignment with reality
- **RIGHT** – Moral integrity and ethical discernment
- **CORRECT** – Balance of technical soundness and contextual precision

Where these two elements intersect is the "zone of wise action."

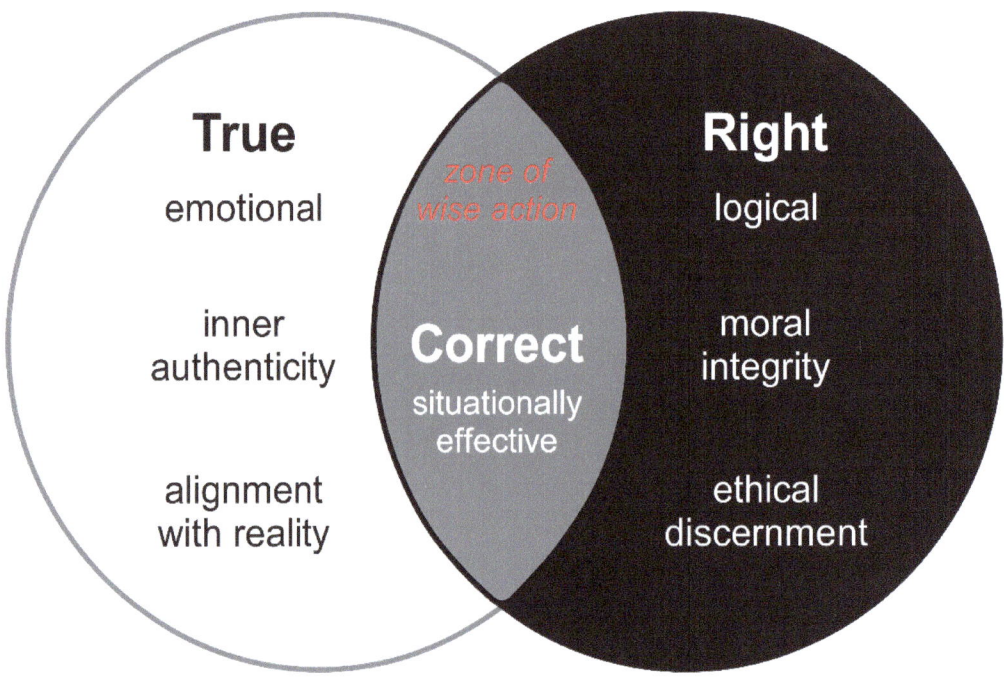

1. TRUE: Alignment with Reality and Authenticity
- **Definition**: What aligns with one's inner values, lived experience, or observable truth
- **Includes**: Self-awareness, factual clarity, personal integrity, intuitive knowing
- **Example**: Expressing a difficult truth even when it's unpopular

Critical Thinking Link: Encourages self-honesty and questions personal assumptions

Reflection Questions:
- Am I being honest with myself and others?
- Is this based on what is real or what is assumed?

- Does this reflect my core values and lived experiences?

2. RIGHT: Moral and Ethical Discernment
- **Definition**: What is just, compassionate, and beneficial from a moral perspective
- **Includes**: Fairness, empathy, justice, long-term benefit to others
- **Example**: Choosing not to exploit a legal loophole because it harms others

Critical Thinking Link: Adds an ethical filter to decisions that might otherwise be purely strategic

Reflection Questions:
- Is this action fair and just?
- Would I consider this acceptable if done to me?
- Does this honor both the letter and spirit of the greater good?

3. CORRECT: The Balance of Functional Precision and Situational Appropriateness
- **Definition**: What is technically accurate, logically coherent, and situationally effective
- **Includes**: Evidence-based reasoning, timing, execution, contextual fit
- **Example**: Using the correct communication method for sensitive feedback

Critical Thinking Link: Embeds the core tools of analysis, logic, and evidence evaluation

Reflection Questions:
- Is this the best balance between true and right, that can serve the most involved?
- Is this method sound and supported by facts?
- Am I choosing the most effective way to act or express this?
- Is it appropriate for this time, place, and audience?

Applications in Teaching and Practice This framework serves as a compass for ethical leadership, personal reflection, and integrative education:
- **In classrooms**: Pairing logic with ethics and introspection
- **In leadership**: Building trust through aligned, values-driven decisions
- **In personal growth**: Assessing decisions using a whole-self model
- **In debate and conflict**: Seeking understanding through multiple lenses

Teaching Module Activities
1. **Case Study Analysis** – Analyze real-world dilemmas from all three perspectives
2. **Personal Journaling** – Reflect on a difficult decision using the lens of true, right, and correct
3. **Group Debates** – Discuss how outcomes shift when one element is missing
4. **Visual Mapping** – Place actions on a Venn diagram to assess alignment

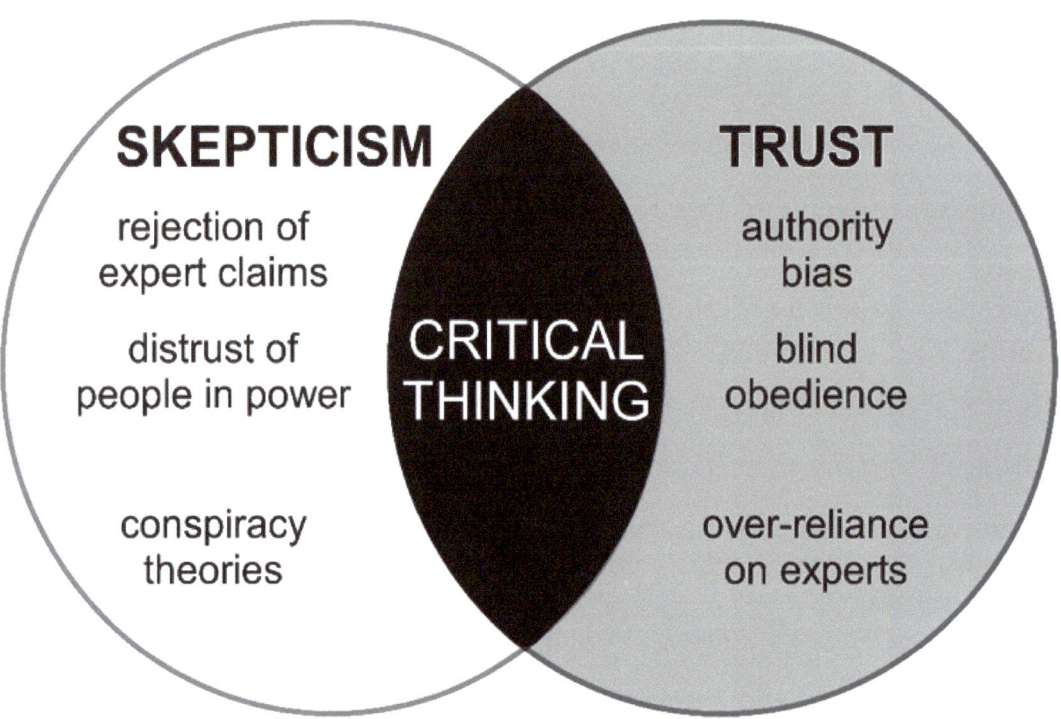

Conclusion The "True, Right, and Correct" framework expands critical thinking into a richer, more human-centered process. It challenges individuals not just to think better, but to *live* and *act* more wisely through authenticity, ethical clarity, and contextual intelligence. In doing so, it reclaims critical thinking not only as a cognitive skill, but as a moral and spiritual practice.

"They Don't Know, What They Don't Know" – The Dunning-Kruger Effect

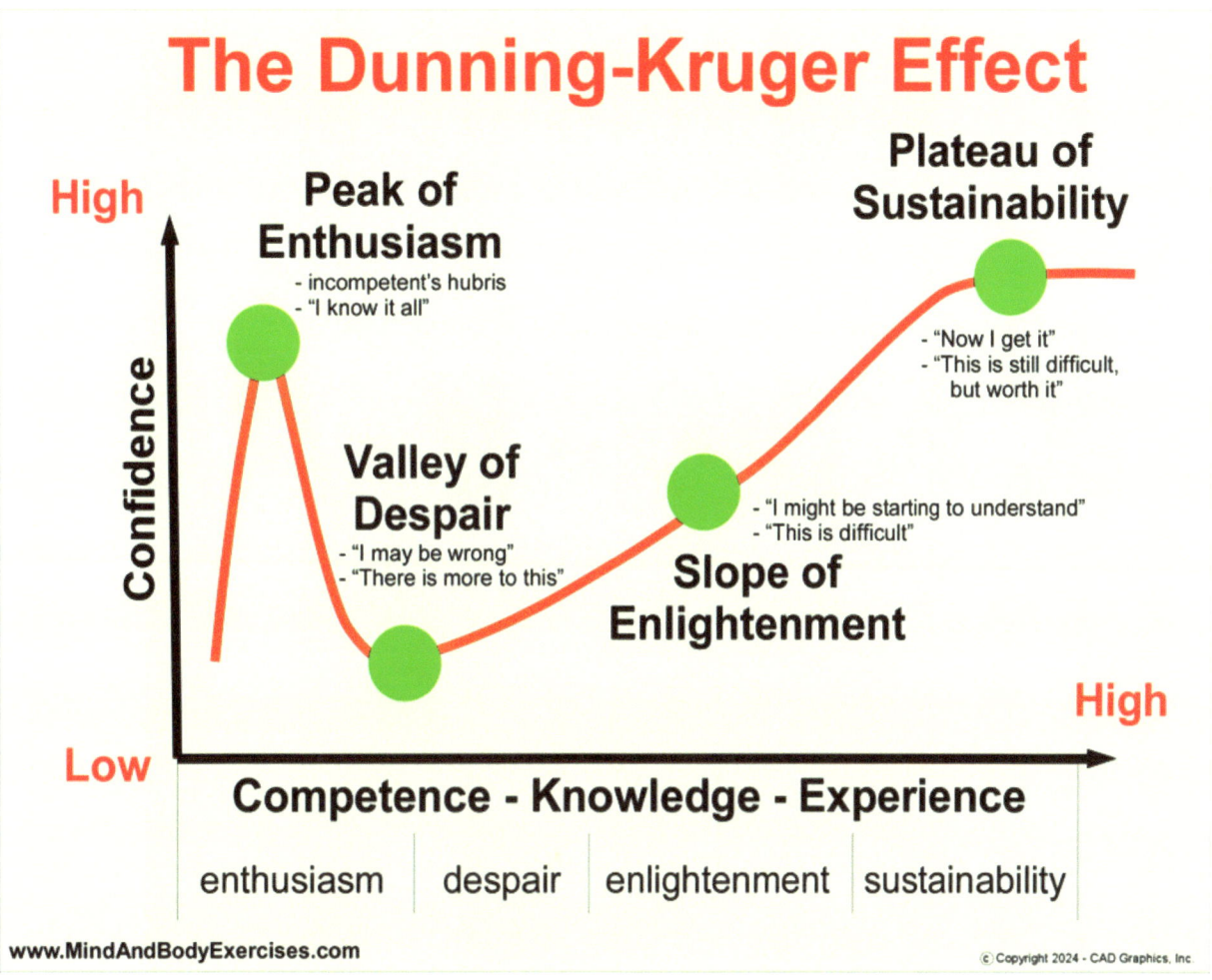

The Dunning-Kruger effect was theorized by psychologists David Dunning and Justin Kruger in a 1999 study. They proposed that there is a cognitive bias where individuals with knowledge or ability within a specific area have a propensity to overestimate their own competence in a particular field. This overestimation may come about due to a lack of the necessary metacognitive skills to accurately determine their own competence.

A common phrase used to summarize this phenomenon is that of *"they don't know, what they don't know."* This effect may be seen in examples of recent high school or college graduates who sometimes express a type of hubris, where they believe that they are intellectually superior to others. Expecting parents sometimes experience this effect where before their child is born, they have delusions of what type of parents they will be. "My kids won't get away with that," "I won't be doing that with my children," or maybe prejudging other parents in how they choose to raise their kids. Once their children are born, new parents might soon realize that parenting is much more complex and difficult than what they first believed.

Hello my name is

Know-it-All

Conversely, those individuals who are highly knowledgeable or skilled in a particular field often underestimate their own competence. This underestimation may manifest because some individuals assume that challenges or projects that are easy for them may also be easy for most others. Well-seasoned individuals in any particular field of knowledge, skill, or ability often gain much wisdom from experience, adaptation, and application of their specific skill set. For some people, this is also highly humbling as the individual realizes that the more someone knows, they ironically recognize that there is so much more to learn.

The Dunning-Kruger effect can be summarized into four key stages:

1. **Incompetence and Confidence:** Individuals possessing low skill levels or knowledge may fail to acknowledge their lack of skill, leading to inflated self-assessments and high confidence.

2. **Awareness of Incompetence:** Once an individual acquires more knowledge and experience, they may start to become more aware of their own incompetence, which in turn leads to a further decrease in confidence.

3. **Competence along with Cautious Confidence:** With further experience, practice, and learning, individuals begin to develop true competence. As their confidence begins to increase again, they can more accurately showcase their abilities.

4. **Mastery with Modesty:** More highly skilled individuals will often acknowledge the complexities of a particular domain and realize how much they still don't know. This awareness can lead to modesty or humbleness about their abilities, despite the individual being highly competent in their specific field.

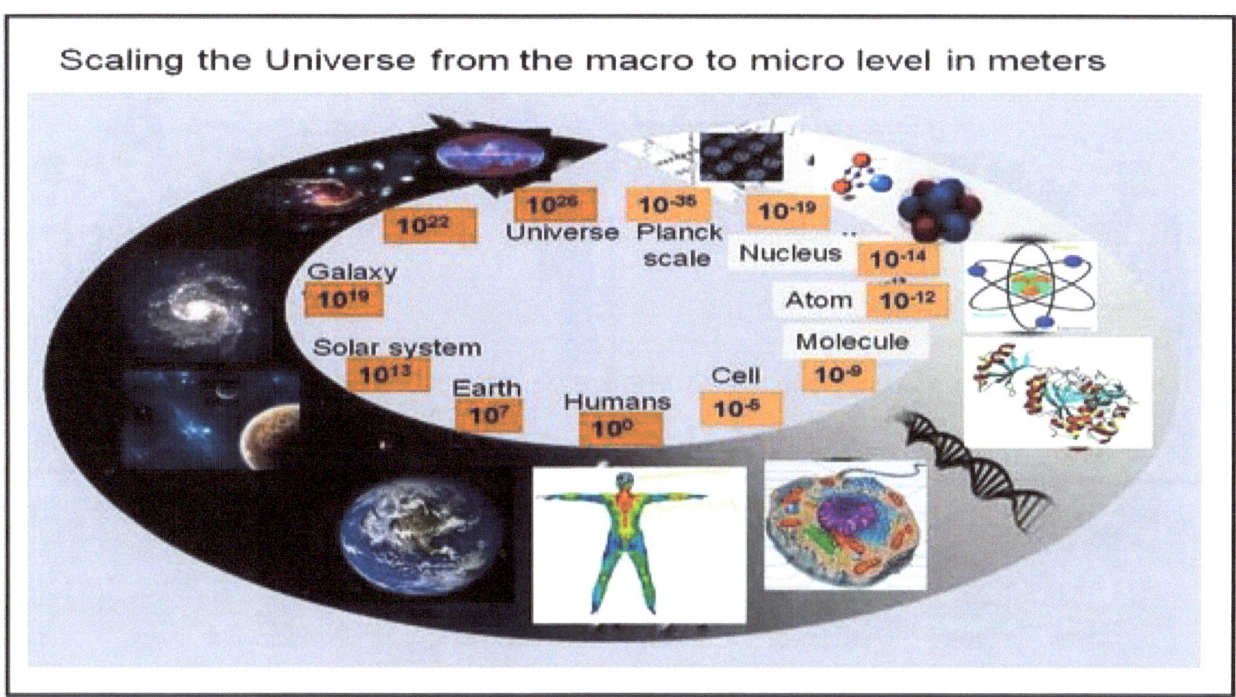

The Dunning-Kruger effect highlights the importance of seeking self-awareness and striving to continue to learn new things. It proposes that improving one's metacognitive skills, such as the ability to self-assess one's own knowledge and performance accurately can help minimize the effect.

In summary, the Dunning-Kruger effect is a cognitive bias where individuals with low knowledge, ability, or competence in a specific area may overestimate their own skill level. On the other hand, people with a high competence in a particular field often underestimate their relative ability. This may occur due to the same skills that contribute to competence also needed to recognize competence, leading to a disconnect between self-assessment and actual ability.

Become the Diamond, Leave the Coal Behind

Humans are like a lump of coal (or carbon), where if put under enough pressure, we may transform into a diamond. I understand that it takes many years, perhaps millions of years, for this transformation to happen. As humans we have only about 70-80 years on average to make our transformation come about, so best to start as soon as possible. I speak of this diamond metaphorically, in regard to each of us being on our own journey to find purpose and meaning in our lives. The diamond is what emerges from the dark and dirty coal, as we strive to find the inner genius, beauty, perfection and acceptance within ourselves.

We all have our own unique set of circumstances with relative trials and tribulations. How we manage these issues are key to our health and happiness. Managing our thoughts, emotions and actions can often be attained from managing our physical body through exercise and deliberate wellness and fitness methods. Qigong (yoga), tai chi, meditation and other methods can offer lifelong benefits to the mind, body and spirit. These practices are paths to become your diamond from the rough of the world.

The process of transforming coal into a diamond takes an incredibly long time—millions to billions of years. Both coal and diamonds are made up of carbon, but the key difference lies in their formation and the conditions under which they are created.

Coal forms from plant material that accumulates in swampy environments over millions of years. Through the process of burial and geological transformation, the organic material undergoes compaction and chemical changes, resulting in the formation of coal. This process typically takes millions of years.

On the other hand, diamonds are formed deep within the Earth's mantle, where high pressure and temperature conditions exist. These conditions cause carbon atoms to arrange in a crystal lattice structure, forming diamonds. This process occurs at depths of around 150 to 200 kilometers (93 to 124 miles) and requires immense pressure and temperatures of approximately 1,000 to 1,300 degrees Celsius (1,832 to 2,372 degrees Fahrenheit). The time required for diamond formation can range from hundreds of millions to billions of years.

Therefore, the transformation of coal into a diamond is an extremely slow and geologically long process, occurring over millions to billions of years under specific conditions deep within the Earth.

Life is a challenge. Nothing worth achieving comes for free. Gifts and rewards are most valuable when earned. Change your coal into diamonds.

Mastery in the World of Form: Integrating Wealth, Health, and Spirit

In the pursuit of personal evolution, many traditions emphasize the renunciation of material wealth as a path to spiritual enlightenment. Yet this view may overlook an essential truth: the mastery of life requires full engagement with both the spiritual and material realms. Rather than rejecting worldly success, a more holistic path invites individuals to develop discipline, embrace responsibility, and integrate spiritual realization with material abundance.

A balanced life requires strength across physical, emotional, and spiritual dimensions. True power, especially in men, is not measured by dominance or accumulation alone, but by maturity and restraint. Without discipline, power can become dangerous, giving rise to instability and harm. Therefore, self-mastery begins with a commitment to personal responsibility, training the body, focusing the mind, and cultivating inner peace.

One foundational concept in this approach is the idea that wealth and health are not opposites of spiritual life but necessary stages in the ladder of awakening. Through conscious acquisition and enjoyment of material pleasures—followed by the ability to release attachment—one gains not only experience but freedom from the cycles of craving and aversion. This path requires mastering the "world of form," learning to participate in it fully without being controlled by it. Those who avoid or bypass this stage may find themselves spiritually incomplete. If one believes in reincarnation, this situation may lead to further experiences in future lifetimes to fully integrate these unlearned lessons.

Conscious development can be mapped through the lens of energy centers or chakras, where each stage corresponds to an essential life lesson: from physical grounding and pleasure to peace, joy, love, compassion, and ultimately ecstatic or blissful states of awareness. These are not mere metaphors but practical tools for tracking one's evolution. A person who cannot access joy or inner peace may need to revisit the foundations of health, safety, and stability before advancing into higher spiritual states.

Seasons of Life - 5 Elements

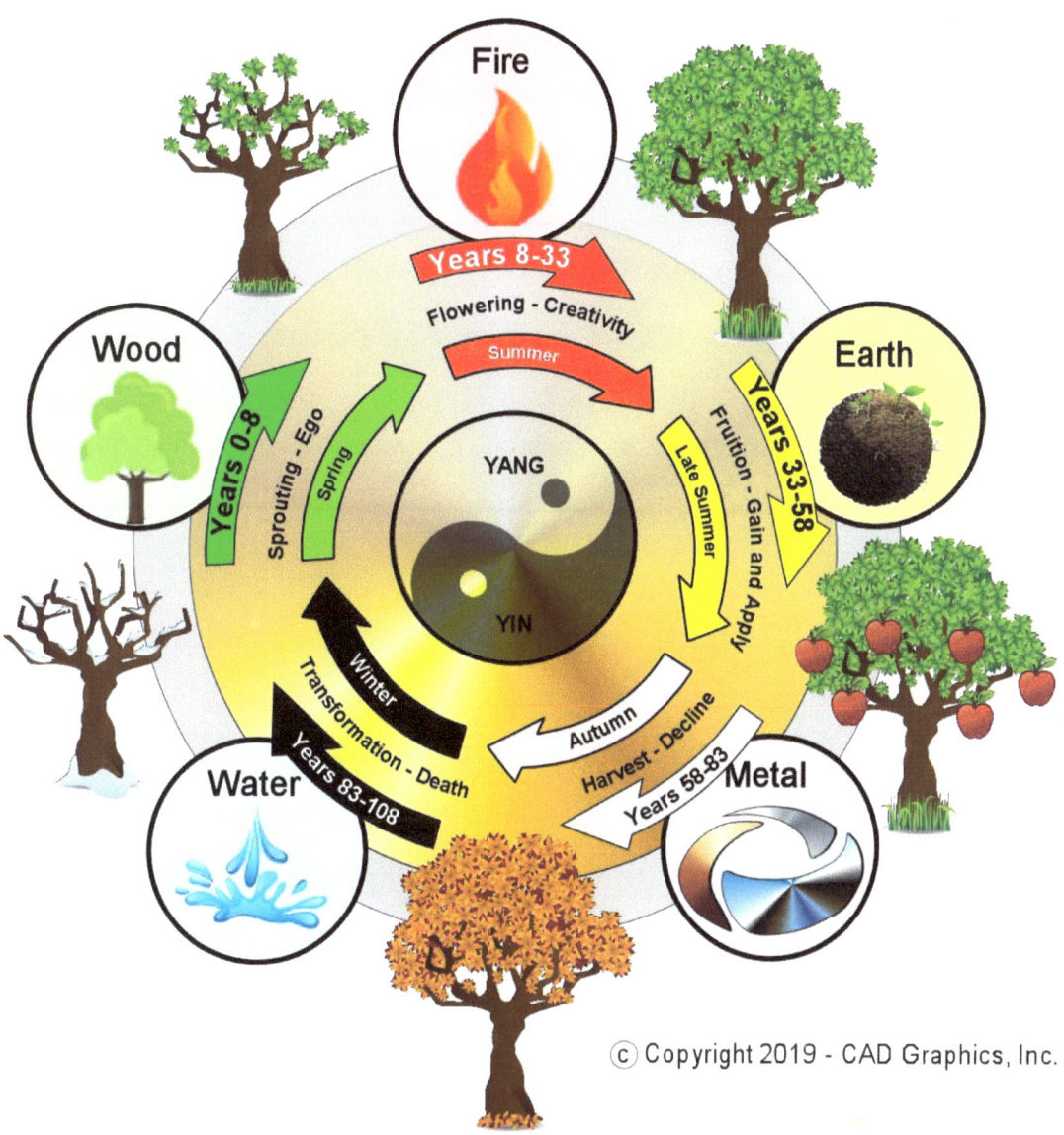

Central to this journey is the rejection of victimhood. Blaming society, circumstances, or others for one's failures hinders growth. Only by accepting full responsibility for one's health, finances, relationships, and spiritual development can one initiate true transformation. This principle applies across life stages, which can be seen as cycles: childhood (0–8), adolescence and young adulthood (8–33), fruition (33–58), correction (58–83), and ultimately the sage or spirit phase (83–108). Each phase carries its own lessons and demands appropriate effort and reflection.

In later life, aging should not be viewed as decay, but as a biological and spiritual opportunity. With proper practice through breathwork, meditation, physical cultivation, and mental clarity, many signs of aging can be reversed or mitigated. The aim is to remain vibrant, focused, and spiritually prepared for death, which, when acknowledged consciously, becomes a motivator for authentic living.

The role of family, lineage, and tradition is also pivotal. Respect for one's parents and ancestors does not require blind obedience or emotional entanglement but calls for honoring their place in one's development. This maturity fosters generational healing and sets an example for those who follow.

Integration of spiritual wisdom with material responsibility is not unique to any one culture. Whether through Christian parables, Taoist discipline, or Buddhist insight, timeless truths emerge: the value of discipline, the importance of presence, the need for compassion, and the certainty of death. When viewed through this inclusive lens, spirituality becomes less about belief and more about the embodiment of universal principles.

The ideal individual, a strong, wise, and compassionate being, embodies the archetype of the strategist and warrior. Not through brute strength or spiritual aloofness, but through the unification of effort, enjoyment, reflection, and humility. Mastery is not found in a cave or an office alone, but in the weaving of both. When one lives fully, without excuses or illusions, the path reveals itself not above the world, but through it.

The Eight Keys of Wisdom

The **Eight Keys of Wisdom** are rooted in **Taoist, Confucian, and Buddhist principles**, such as:
- **Wu Wei (Effortless Action)** in Taoism, similar to "Be Like Bamboo" (flexibility and balance).
- **Right Conduct and Ethics** in Confucianism, similar to "The True-Right-Correct Method."
- **Mindfulness and Detachment from Thought** in Buddhism are reflected in "Stop Being Drunk on Your Own Thoughts."

The **Eight Keys of Wisdom** serve as guiding principles for integrating mindfulness and meditation into daily life. Here's a deeper look at each:

1. Reflection (Know Your True Self)
- This key emphasizes self-awareness and authenticity.

- It encourages recognizing personal strengths, weaknesses, and emotional patterns.
- Understanding oneself allows for conscious decision-making and alignment with one's true nature.

2. Make Correct Choices (The True-Right-Correct Method)
- Rooted in Eastern philosophy, this principle teaches the importance of seeking truth and making ethical choices.
- "True" represents inner wisdom, "Right" signifies ethical action, and "Correct" ensures that actions align with both personal integrity and universal balance.

3. Overcome Delusion (Stop Being Drunk on Your Own Thoughts)
- Encourages detachment from overthinking and emotional reactivity.
- Teaches mindfulness techniques to observe thoughts without being consumed by them.
- Helps develop clarity and inner calm by breaking free from habitual negative thinking.

4. How Will You Be Remembered? (Plant Good Seeds)
- Invites reflection on one's legacy and the impact of actions on others.
- Encourages living with purpose, kindness, and awareness of how one's presence affects the world.
- Turn on your light, becoming an inspiration and not a warning to others

5. Seek Connectedness & Honor (Be Like a Mountain)
- Focuses on building meaningful relationships through respect, integrity, and compassion.
- Recognizes the interconnectedness of all people and the importance of honoring those connections.
- Teaches that true strength comes from unity rather than isolation.

6. Change Your Reality for the Better
- Encourages personal responsibility in shaping one's experiences.
- Highlights the power of perspective—choosing optimism and proactive behavior over victimhood.
- Teaches how shifting internal attitudes can influence external circumstances.

7. Become a Vessel of Wisdom (It Only Takes One Match to Light a Thousand)
- Demonstrates the power of small actions in creating widespread change.
- Encourages leading by example, where one positive act can inspire many others.
- Stresses that transformation begins with individual effort, no matter how small.

8. Draw from Nature's Energies (Be Like Bamboo)
- Symbolizes resilience, flexibility, and strength.
- Encourages adaptability in the face of challenges while maintaining inner strength.
- Teaches that true power lies in balance, being strong yet flexible, firm yet yielding.

The **Eight Keys of Wisdom** are rooted in **Taoist, Confucian, and Buddhist principles**, such as:
- **Wu Wei (Effortless Action)** in Taoism, similar to "Be Like Bamboo" (flexibility and balance).
- **Right Conduct and Ethics** in Confucianism, similar to "The True-Right-Correct Method."
- **Mindfulness and Detachment from Thought** in Buddhism are reflected in "Stop Being Drunk on Your Own Thoughts."

D: Emotional Intelligence & Healing from Trauma

Seek Out the "Wounded Healers"

Would you seek dental help from a dentist with rotten teeth?

Ask for relationship advice from someone that has a record of domestic abuse?

Take your car to a mechanic whose own automobile is always broken down?

Then why would you seek advice on health and well-being from someone who themselves is not healthy and well?

I have previously come across the concept of the "wounded healer." There is no shortage of books and articles on this topic, where people that have first-hand experience with surviving trauma are often the best empaths for a particular issue. Psychologist Carl Jung may have been the first to use this term back in 1951, where he proposed that disease of the soul could be the most advantageous type of training for a healer. Jung was thought to believe that only a wounded physician could heal effectively. An empath that truly understands another's circumstances may be of great benefit and perhaps provide a guided path to post-traumatic growth (PTG). PTG is the term for what happens when someone who struggles psychologically from trauma and adversity, comes to experience positive, transformative changes in their mindset and behavior. "Finding the silver lining in all things, good or bad," is a quote many of us are quite familiar with.

How can something "good" come from things that are seemingly "bad?" While I don't think anyone truly looks forward to any personal loss and/or suffering on any level, there are sometimes good aspects that can come out of even the worst of circumstances. Losses or misfortunes can offer the possibility of life-enhancing "post-traumatic growth" as someone weaves the lessons of loss and resilience into their life moving forward. Personal growth following major experiences of loss is common (Hall, 2014). From my experiences in teaching fitness, wellness, and mindfulness, I have found most people do not have a deeper connection to their own health, well-being, or consciousness until some event of trauma as a life-threatening or life-changing situation enters into their life.

Loss of life of a family member or close friend can be the spark that causes another to change their behaviors. Someone passing of a heart attack at an early age, might motivate others to watch their own health closer. Mental or physical trauma can sometimes lead to what some call "knowing one's true self", self-realization or enlightenment. Taoism and Buddhism has taught me decades ago, that trauma can be means to knowing one's true self. Trauma can be very intense and life-changing experiences that an individual may become so affected that they may appear to others to have evolved overnight into a different person. Many of us have encountered someone who while in dire straits, promises to change their ways if their circumstances where to play out in their favor. Changes of this sort can be viewed as positive or negative, as all things are relative. Change through motivation, stemming from trauma.

I have discussed alcoholism in some of my past posts here, as it is a topic that I am quite familiar with. We can see the wounded healer here, where survivors of alcoholism or those who have experienced alcohol abuse-related relationships often have firsthand experience with coping with alcohol related issues. Similarly, survivors of abusive relationships and varying levels of trauma have been wounded themselves but can also help others to heal by extending empathy and, if sought, advice. This same concept may hold validity for survivors of law enforcement related events, survivors of war trauma as soldiers and/or civilians, healthcare workers, firefighters and many others involved in service to others. However, in order to serve effectively as a wounded healer, this individual needs to be able to manage their own stress, suffering and other mental and physical ailments before extending their advice to others that are suffering. Otherwise, this individual, while having good intentions, may actually come off as being less understanding, less empathetical and perhaps hypocritical, and therefore causing more harm to a sufferer.

(1) Survivors of alcoholism or those who have experienced alcohol abuse-related relationships

(2) Survivors of abusive relationships on all levels of trauma

(3) Survivors of violence and/or law enforcement related events

(4) Survivors of war trauma as soldiers and/or civilians

(5) Survivors from cults and other particular groups

(6) Survivors of physical accidents or catastrophe

References:

Daneault S. The wounded healer: can this idea be of use to family physicians? Can Fam Physician. 2008 Sep;54(9):1218-9, 1223-5. PMID: 18791082; PMCID: PMC2553448.

https://www.azquotes.com/quote/1200463

Hall, C. (2014). Bereavement theory: recent developments in our understanding of grief and bereavement. Bereavement Care, 33(1), 7–12.
https://doi.org/10.1080/02682621.2014.902610

Unseen Wounds: How Emotional Trauma Shapes Our Health

Despite living in an age of advanced medicine and rising health awareness, chronic illness, emotional suffering, and addiction continue to rise. This contradiction invites us to question not just our treatments but also the mindset and motivation behind them. Increasingly, research and lived experience point to unprocessed pain and trauma as the core drivers of both psychological and physiological illness.

Medicine's Narrow Focus: Suppressing Symptoms Instead of Healing

Contemporary medical practices often focus on symptom suppression rather than root-cause healing. For example, elevated cortisol, a hormone associated with stress, is frequently managed with pharmaceuticals that reduce inflammation but fail to address the underlying source of distress (Sapolsky, 2004). In cases of chronic illness, especially cancer, mainstream interventions often fall back on drastic methods: cutting (surgery), poisoning (chemotherapy), or burning (radiation), with minimal inquiry into psychosomatic or emotional contributors.

The pharmaceutical industry has also come under scrutiny for prioritizing profit-driven solutions that treat stress biochemically without offering tools for actual emotional or relational healing (Gabor Maté, 2010).

A Society Obsessed with Health Yet Unwell

We live in a paradoxical society: obsessed with fitness, diet, and health optimization, yet disconnected from authentic well-being. Emotional pain is frequently seen as a personal failure, and expressions of vulnerability are often equated with weakness. Shame becomes a hidden driver of behavior, shaping identity through internalized messages like "I'm not enough" or "My needs don't matter" (Brown, 2012).

The metaphor of the "monster" within, like the transformation of Bruce Banner into the Hulk, illustrates how repressed emotions can erupt when unacknowledged. We often assume that other people's issues are about us, leading to further internal conflict and disconnection.

Trauma: The Root Cause of Addiction and Illness

Pain, especially unresolved emotional pain, is at the root of many afflictions. According to trauma expert Gabor Maté (2008), addiction is not a disease or choice but a response to deep suffering. Whether through substances, work, food, or achievement, people are often trying to soothe pain they may not even fully understand.

Social disconnection, abandonment, and lack of emotional education perpetuate trauma across generations. Society offers little support or guidance for managing grief, shame, or stress. Many turn to coping mechanisms without the tools to process their trauma, which is especially evident in marginalized communities where chronic stress is linked to disproportionately higher rates of illness (Williams & Mohammed, 2009).

The Cost of Disconnection and the Need for Authenticity

In professional fields like medicine, unresolved trauma is common. Some individuals pursue high-achieving careers not from passion but to compensate for feelings of inadequacy or unlovability. Emotional detachment, often a survival strategy in childhood, becomes normalized in adulthood. This disconnection between ***mind and body*** leads to chronic stress, illness, and burnout (Van der Kolk, 2014).

Authentic healing requires honoring two essential human needs: **attachment** and **authenticity**. When these needs are in conflict, as they often are in trauma survivors, authenticity is usually sacrificed for the sake of relational survival. Reconnecting with one's truth, expressing anger constructively, and embracing emotional honesty are key steps toward transformation.

Healing the Generational Wounds

Trauma doesn't disappear. It is often passed from one generation to the next, not just through genetics but through behavior, belief systems, and emotional suppression. Children absorb the stress of their caregivers. Without awareness and intervention, these patterns replicate over time (Yehuda & Lehrner, 2018).

What may appear as weakness, in hypervigilance, dissociation, emotional volatility, is often a response to longstanding unmet needs. Healing begins by naming these patterns and allowing space for expression and integration.

A Shift Toward Integration and Compassion

The healing path is not just clinical, it is relational, emotional, and spiritual. Psychedelic-assisted therapy, somatic practices, plant medicines like *ayahuasca*, and trauma-informed psychotherapy are gaining traction because they center empathy, connection, and emotional truth (Carhart-Harris & Goodwin, 2017).

As we reevaluate addiction, trauma, and illness through this lens, we begin to see that these challenges are not signs of brokenness. Rather, they are indicators of what needs acknowledgment, healing, and reintegration. Addiction, far from being a moral failure or inherited defect, can be seen as a solution to an emotional problem, a cry for help that must be understood before it can be addressed.

References

Brown, B. (2012). DARING GREATLY. In *GOTHAM BOOKS*. GOTHAM BOOKS. https://site.ieee.org/sb-nhce/files/2021/06/Brene-brown-book1.pdf

Carhart-Harris, R. L., & Goodwin, G. M. (2017). The therapeutic potential of psychedelic drugs: Past, present, and future. *Neuropsychopharmacology*, 42(11), 2105–2113. https://doi.org/10.1038/npp.2017.84

Maté, G. (2008). *In the realm of hungry ghosts: Close encounters with addiction*. Knopf Canada. https://drgabormate.com/book/in-the-realm-of-hungry-ghosts/

Maté, G. (2010). *When the body says no: The cost of hidden stress*. Wiley. When the Body Says No - Dr. Gabor Maté

Sapolsky, R. (2004). Why Zebras don't get Ulcers: The acclaimed Guide to Stress, Stress-Related Diseases, and Coping. *ResearchGate*. https://www.researchgate.net/publication/272161275_Why_Zebras_Don't_Get_Ulcers_The_Acclaimed_Guide_to_Stress_Stress-Related_Diseases_and_Coping

Van der Kolk, B. (2014). *The body keeps the score: Brain, mind, and body in the healing of trauma*. Viking. The body keeps the score: Brain, mind, and body in the healing of trauma.

Williams, D. R., & Mohammed, S. A. (2009). Discrimination and racial disparities in health: Evidence and needed research. *Journal of Behavioral Medicine*, 32(1), 20–47. https://doi.org/10.1007/s10865-008-9185-0

Yehuda, R., & Lehrner, A. (2018). Intergenerational transmission of trauma effects: Putative role of epigenetic mechanisms. *World Psychiatry*, 17(3), 243–257. https://doi.org/10.1002/wps.20568

The Misogi Challenge

A Modern Rite of Passage for Mind, Body, and Spirit

In today's comfort-saturated world, we often forget what we're capable of. We live behind screens, within routines, and beneath our potential. But what if, once a year, you did something so challenging, so outrageous that it forced you to face your limits and break through them? That's the spirit of "***Misogi***."

What Is Misogi?

Misogi is an ancient *Shinto* purification ritual originating in Japan. Traditionally performed under icy waterfalls or in natural bodies of water, it involves cold-water immersion, breath control, and chanting to wash away impurities, not just physical dirt, but emotional, mental, and spiritual stagnation. It's about cleansing the soul, aligning with nature, and stepping into renewed awareness.

"Misogi is not about strength; it's about sincerity." – Japanese proverb

From Ritual to Challenge: The Modern Misogi

In recent years, Misogi has evolved beyond religious rituals into a deliberate act of voluntary hardship. Misogi is a physical and mental challenge that reclaims the spirit of transformation. Spearheaded by thinkers like Dr. Marcus Elliott, the modern Misogi is a once-a-year event so difficult that there's a 50% chance of failure.

The Rules of Modern Misogi:

1. It should be physically and/or mentally extreme.
2. There should be a real risk of not finishing.
3. No audience. This is not for social media likes.
4. It should change one's perspective on the way you see the rest of their life.

Holistic Health Benefits of Misogi

From a holistic wellness standpoint, the Misogi Challenge is more than a test of will, it's a full-spectrum recalibration:

Mental Fortitude

Pushing beyond perceived limits activates the prefrontal cortex, engages deep concentration, and can restructure your relationship with fear and discomfort (Tse et al., 2007).

Physical Resilience

Strenuous, unfamiliar tasks force the body to adapt, strengthen, and detoxify, stimulating lymphatic flow, cardiovascular function, and musculoskeletal balance (Nieman, 2003).

Energetic Alignment

Like cold plunges in Taoist and Ayurvedic cleansing rituals, Misogi resets energetic flow (*Qi* or *prana*), breaking through stagnation that can lead to disease (Larre et al., 1996).

Spiritual Renewal

Letting go of the ego, expectations, and habitual comforts creates space for inner clarity and reconnection to purpose. It becomes a form of sacred self-inquiry.

Designing a Misogi Challenge for Different Wellness Levels

Seniors or Holistic Wellness Groups

- **Challenge**: 12-hour digital fast with 6-hour silent walking meditation
- **Why**: Encourages mindfulness, self-awareness, and reconnection with breath and body
- **Modify with**: Journaling and gentle breathwork (e.g., qigong or walking tai chi)

Moderate Fitness Level

- **Challenge**: 20-mile nature hike with water-only fasting
- **Why**: Combines physical exertion, solitude, and environmental reconnection
- **Modify with**: Breaks for seated meditation or breath practice every 5 miles

Advanced Practitioners or Athletes

- **Challenge**: Carrying a heavy object (rock, sandbag) across natural terrain for 2–3 hours in silence

- **Why**: Deeply tests body and mind under primal conditions
- **Modify with**: Incorporate chants, breath pacing, or visualization

Integration Is Key

A true Misogi doesn't end when the task is complete. The reflection period is just as important:

- Journal about what arose emotionally and physically
- Meditate on what you let go of and what you discovered
- Ask yourself: *Who was I before this, and who am I now?*

Misogi in the Modern World

While Misogi may sound extreme, it addresses a modern spiritual hunger or the need for voluntary adversity (strategic trauma) that leads to inner growth. We lack rites of passage in our society, and so our transformation remains stunted. Misogi reclaims this space and offers a framework for regeneration, not just resilience.

In the end, Misogi isn't about conquest. It's about coming clean with your body, your breath, your fears, and your forgotten strength. Misogi is less about proving you can finish and more about remembering what's possible when you try.

Even once a year, stepping into something so bold, uncomfortable, and transformative can reset your relationship with fear, complacency, and the stories you tell yourself. Misogi is a sacred dare to become fully alive.

Last year, I committed to a 3-month rigorous physical training regimen to prepare for a 10-day hiking expedition across Utah's Mighty Five national parks. A journey that demanded not only endurance but also mental clarity and emotional resilience. In many ways, it became my own version of a Misogi Challenge.

Drawing from decades of experience in Tai Chi, Qigong, and other time-tested fitness and wellness systems, I developed a holistic training protocol that addressed balance, breath, posture, flexibility, and mindset. This integrative approach not only strengthened my body for the miles ahead but also deepened my presence and appreciation for the journey itself.

I now help others design their own *Misogi-style challenges*, whether it's a hiking goal, a fitness milestone, or a personal rite of passage, using adaptable practices rooted in Eastern movement arts and modern wellness science. You don't need to be an elite athlete; you only need the willingness to step beyond comfort and toward transformation.

References

Larre, C., de la Vallée, E., & Rochat de la Vallée, E. (1996). *The Eight Extraordinary Meridians: Spirit of the Vessels*. Monkey Press.

Nieman, D. C. (2003). Current perspective on exercise immunology. *Current Sports Medicine Reports*, *2*(5), 239–242. https://doi.org/10.1249/00149619-200310000-00001

Tse, D., Langston, R. F., Kakeyama, M., Bethus, I., Spooner, P. A., Wood, E. R., ... & Morris, R. G. (2007). Schemas and memory consolidation. *Science, 316*(5821), 76-82. https://doi.org/10.1126/science.1135935

URI: The Language of Togetherness Across Cultures

In Korean culture, one of the most powerful words is also one of the simplest: **Uri,** meaning "we" or "our." But Uri is far more than a pronoun. It is a window into how Koreans understand relationships, group identity, and emotional belonging. Within traditional Korean martial arts circles, especially under the guidance of masters who emphasize discipline and loyalty, Uri is often used to describe the unshakable camaraderie and shared identity between students and instructors, forged through hardship, challenge, and growth.

Uri: More Than "We"

In English, "we" is often just a grammatical term, used to distinguish from "I" or "you." But in Korean, Uri is embedded deeply in the language and mindset, often used even when referring to something that belongs to oneself:

- *uri jip – our house*, not *my house*
- *uri eomma – our mom*, not *my mom*
- *uri hakgyo – our school*, not *my school*

This reflects a collectivist worldview in which individuals see themselves as part of a larger whole, whether that's a family, class, team, or nation (Kim & Choi, 1994).

In martial arts dojangs (training halls), Uri expresses more than membership; it expresses loyalty, mutual care, and emotional bonding. When a teacher speaks of "our students" or "our school," it reinforces unity and shared responsibility.

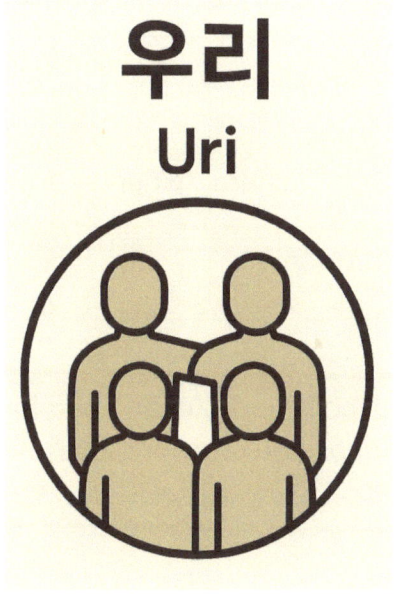

Uri and Jeong: The Emotional Core

Complementing Uri is the concept of *Jeong*, a deep, enduring emotional bond that forms over time through shared life, hardship, and loyalty. Jeong isn't easily expressed in words. It shows up in quiet sacrifice, remembered favors, unspoken forgiveness, and decades of unwavering care (Kim, 2025).

In the martial arts setting, Jeong may grow silently between a student and teacher over years of training, discipline, and shared struggle. It does not need to be spoken, it is understood.

So, while Uri reflects group identity, Jeong is the emotional glue within that group.

Related Cultural Concepts

Korea's rich cultural emphasis on relational harmony and group belonging has echoes in neighboring traditions:

Concept	Culture	Meaning
Uri (우리)	Korean	"We" / "Our" - shared identity and belonging
Jeong (정)	Korean	Emotional bond of affection and loyalty
Qíng (情)	Chinese	Sentiment, emotion in social and familial roles (Li, 2016)
Rénqing (人情)	Chinese	Social etiquette, reciprocal human feelings (Yan, 1996)
Camaraderie	American/Western	Friendly solidarity from shared experiences
Brotherhood/Sisterhood	Universal	Loyalty forged through common hardship

While these concepts vary, they all point to a human need for belonging, connection, and emotional safety, particularly in groups bound by purpose, like martial arts, military service, or community living.

Uri in the Dojang: A Warrior's Bond

In martial arts, Uri reflects a mindset of shared struggle and mutual respect. It means:

- We endure hardship together
- We uphold the dignity of the group, not just the self
- We protect and support each other in and out of training

A Korean master might speak of Uri when referring to the lineage, the school's mission, or the bond between instructors and students who have faced hardship side-by-side.

Even in moments of silence, when no words are spoken, Uri is felt, in a bowed head, a shared meal, or the gentle correction of a form done poorly but with heart.

Uri vs. Western Individualism

Western cultures often emphasize personal agency, independence, and distinct identity ("I did it," "my house," "my success"). In contrast, Uri reflects a Korean cultural mindset in which the group defines the individual, not the other way around.

This is not about erasing personal identity, but rather about honoring relationships as central to identity.

Conclusion: Uri as a Way of Life

In the end, Uri is more than a word. It is a cultural philosophy, one that holds that we are strongest together, that emotional ties matter, and that belonging is essential to the human experience. In a martial arts context, it is the thread that weaves through every bowed head, every shared hardship, every correction given with care.

As we compare Uri with concepts like Jeong, Qing, and camaraderie, we discover that while the language may differ, the longing for connection is universal. The Korean term Uri offers us a powerful lens through which to reexamine not just how we speak, but how we live, with and for each other.

References:

Kim, J. K. (2025). Deconstructing the Marginalized Self: A Homiletical Theology of URI for the Korean American Protestant Church in the Multicultural American context. *Religions*, *16*(2), 249. https://doi.org/10.3390/rel16020249

Kim, U., & Choi, S.-H. (1994). Individualism, collectivism, and child development: A Korean perspective. In P. M. Greenfield & R. R. Cocking (Eds.), *Cross-cultural roots of minority child development* (pp. 227–257). Lawrence Erlbaum Associates, Inc.

Li, J. (2023). *Confucian affect (Qing 情) as the foundation for mutual care and moral elevation*. https://philarchive.org/rec/LICAQM

Yan, Y. (1996). *The Flow of Gifts: Reciprocity and Social Networks in a Chinese Village*. Stanford University Press.

E: Cultural Commentary & Social Reflections

Wealth Without Wellness is Poverty in Disguise

No Amount of Wealth, Status, or Celebrity Can Take the Place of a Neglected Mind and Body

In an age where wealth, fame, and social standing are glorified as the pinnacle of success, it is easy to forget that the most valuable assets we possess are not in our bank accounts or in our résumés. Rather they are the state of our minds and the vitality of our bodies. Material fortune and public recognition can buy influence, open doors, and offer fleeting pleasures, but they cannot reverse years of physical neglect or restore a mind dulled by stress, apathy, or overindulgence. The truth is simple: when the mind and body are compromised, the currency of wealth and the applause of the crowd lose their meaning.

The Illusion of Substitution

Society often promotes the illusion that money, influence, or fame can make up for a lack of health. We see celebrities celebrated despite visible physical decline, business leaders pushing themselves past the brink of exhaustion, and influencers curating glamorous online lives while privately battling anxiety, burnout, and chronic illness. This image of "success" hides a grim reality. No amount of financial or social power can purchase a new nervous system, undo the damage of decades of poor lifestyle habits, or replace the inner peace that comes from a well-cared-for mind.

Wealth can buy advanced medical treatment, but it cannot buy resilience built from consistent exercise, balanced nutrition, and quality rest. It can hire therapists and coaches, but it cannot magically instill mental clarity, discipline, or emotional stability in a person unwilling to nurture them. It can provide luxury and comfort, but it cannot offer the satisfaction of living in a body and mind that are strong, agile, and alert.

The Human Cost of Neglect

Neglect of the body often begins subtly. Skipped workouts, poor sleep, diets based on convenience rather than nutrition and other issues emerge as seemingly harmless lapses. Over time, this neglect compounds where muscles and bones weaken, cardiovascular endurance drops, weight accumulates, and chronic conditions take root. The body, once ignored, demands attention in ways that money alone cannot silence. Arthritis cannot be bribed. A failing heart cannot be impressed by prestige. The slow erosion of mobility and vitality spares no one.

Similarly, the neglected mind suffers in ways that wealth cannot mend. Without continuous learning, mental challenges, and emotional self-regulation, the mind becomes less adaptable. Stress becomes more overwhelming, decision-making more erratic, and creativity more stagnant. Intellectual and emotional atrophy often occur long before physical decline becomes visible, robbing life of richness and depth.

Real Wealth: Mind-Body Integrity

The most enduring form of success comes from balance: a mind that remains curious, clear, and resilient, and a body that can carry us through life's challenges with strength and endurance. This integrity cannot be purchased, but rather it must be cultivated through daily choices. Physical exercise strengthens not just the body but also mental health, reducing anxiety and improving cognitive function. Mindful practices such as meditation, reflection, and deliberate learning sharpen awareness and emotional stability. Proper nutrition fuels both the brain and the muscles, enabling them to function at their best.

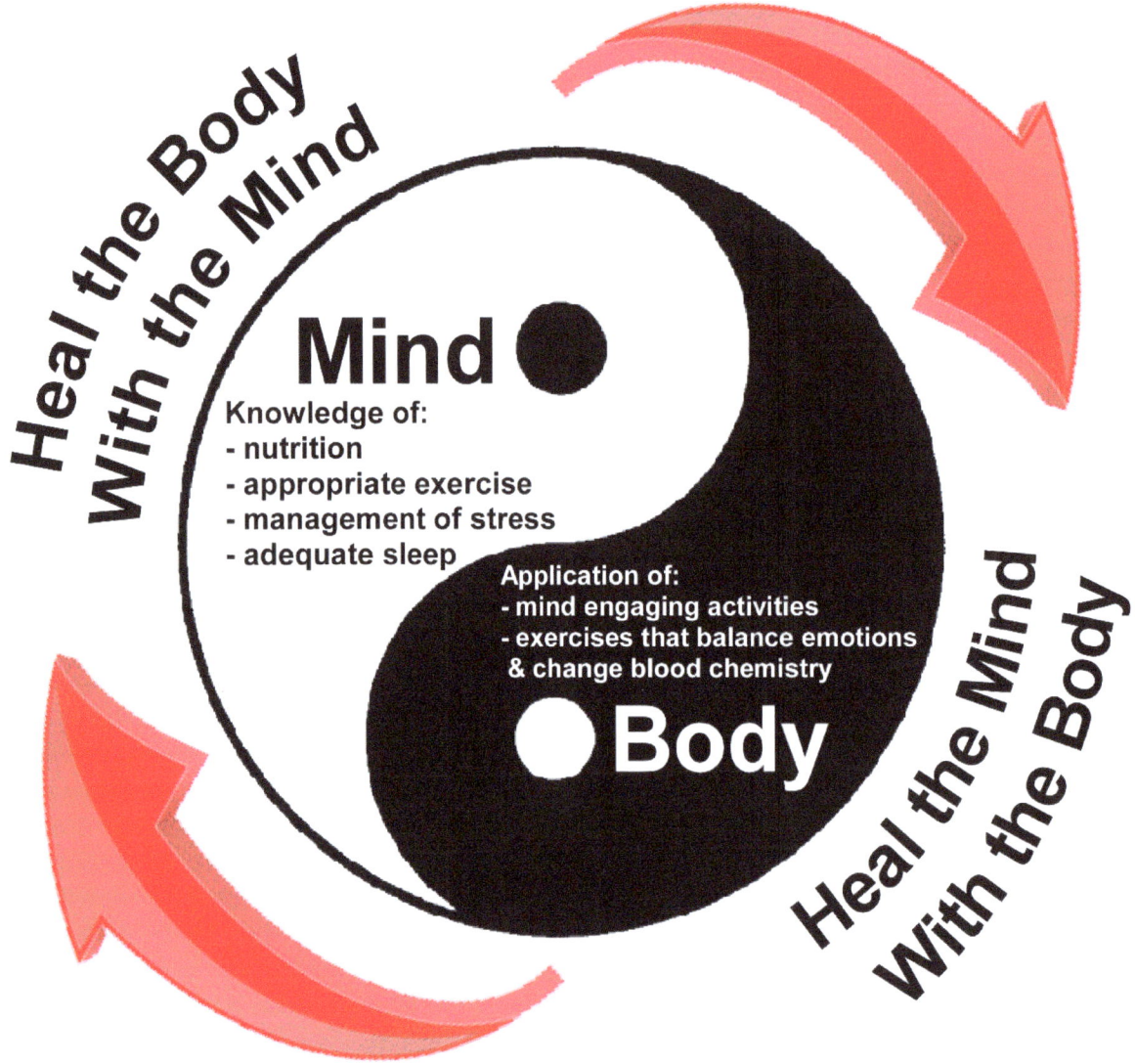

True prestige comes from being able to meet each day's demands with clarity of thought, steadiness of emotion, and physical capability. A billionaire confined by illness envies the healthy freedom of someone who can walk without pain. A public figure struggling with depression or mental exhaustion would trade their followers for peace of mind. In the end, health is the foundation upon which all other forms of success are built. ***Good Health is Wealth.***

Lessons from History and Life

History offers countless examples of individuals whose material success could not shield them from the consequences of neglect. Famous industrialists, politicians, and entertainers have succumbed to preventable diseases, addictions, and burnout. Some reached the heights of their careers only to spend their later years consumed by medical treatments or emotional turmoil. On the other hand, there are those of modest means who lived into old age with vibrant energy and mental clarity, not because they had wealth or fame, but because they respected and maintained their inner and outer well-being.

Conclusion: The Non-Negotiable Priority

In the end, the message is clear: a neglected mind and body will undermine every other achievement. Wealth and status are fleeting. The body and mind are the constant companions that shape every moment of experience. Taking care of them is not an optional luxury. A strong and healthy mind, as well as physical body are the foundation for a life well-lived. The most successful person is not necessarily the one with the most accolades or the largest bank account, but the one who can wake each day with the energy to act, the clarity to think, and the inner peace to enjoy the journey.

No title, no fortune, no spotlight can take the place of that.

Do Recreational Sports and Religions Exist in Separate Domains?

Americans do love their sports, as do many other nations and their populations across the world. America has about 29% of the population considered as avid fans and 46% as casual fans (Statista, 2023). Another source reports that Americans consider themselves sports fans in general at 63% versus Europeans at 69% (YPulse, 2023). I surmise that there are many other studies and reports on this topic that will sway far and wide depending upon the researchers and intent for the studies. I think this is important to note due to the question of separation between sports and religion. Additionally, I do think that many Americans feel that they do not have to have an affiliation to sports or religion, where the two can very much be mutually exclusive of each other. Or, where either of these two elements of American culture are related in ways that would make the others incompatible or null to the other. Many do not want to see their own involvement in sports, on any level to be labeled as a religious relationship.

However, when analyzed for specific similarities in components of various religions, such as rituals, initiations, use of symbols, conformity to the group and groupthink, superstitions, adherence to uniforms/clothing/hairstyle, and particular jargon, sports fans often have all these boxes checked. So do many branches of the military in the US and worldwide. Many of these facets exist in liminal groups of particular sects and brotherhoods (Kottak, 2019). Ironically, these components are often the same criteria that are evaluated in labeling particular groups as cults or cult-like. "Culture" is often used for more positive contexts. "Cult" is a word that gathers a much more negative response. Being labeled as a cult can have significant consequences for any religious institution, sports team/group, or various other groups and their members, even in countries that are openly committed to religious freedom and freedom of speech (Peretz, et al., 2021).

This topic of recreational activities and religions strikes a nerve with me as I have had firsthand experience and knowledge, in participation within various groups that have received the "cult" label. Church groups (Christianity, Taoism, Scientology), sports teams/groups/fans (baseball, football, cheerleading, rowing), and fitness trends (martial arts, yoga, Falun gong) have all been labeled to outsiders of these groups as cults on some levels large and small. Consequently, I have come to understand that one person's culture is another person's cult. Similarly, one person's sport may be seen as religious to others not in that group.

I do think that a benefit and disadvantage of modern society is the need to assign a label to every single thing, big and small, animate and inanimate, real or imagined, etc. While striving to have clear definitions for all things, we often fail in the realization that not everything is either black or white, or absolute. Rather, all things are in a constant state of flux and/or change, relative to their unique set of circumstances at a given time and place. People in Salem were labeled as witches and burned to death a few hundred years ago. Religious groups worldwide still to this day kill one another to prove who is more righteous. While the US does have its many problems, fortunately, we do have these sometimes-considered pesky little words of the 1st amendment that allow us the right to express ourselves rather in speech, freedom to worship, or freedom to be fanatical in sports and recreation activities as long as it does not infringe upon another's rights.

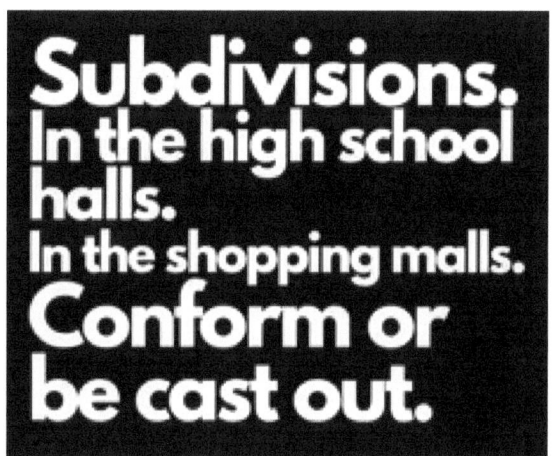

Someone may enjoy watching or participating in sports activities but does not necessarily need to be a fan(atic). Similarly again, not all religions need to be labeled as cults, nor are all cults religious. Much grey area as everyone is free to have their own perspectives on these issues here in the US, for now at least. Some places elsewhere in the world cannot even openly engage in this conversation. Sports and religion, despite their similarities, serve different roles in society and culture. Therefore, I agree that religion and recreation can be separated.

Religion	Sports	Boy/Girl Scouts	Military Service
start events with standing, kneeling, songs	standing and singing songs	Songs for entertainment	Songs during training
chants, spells, calling ons luck or divine	chants, calling on luck, prayers luck or divine	prayers	individual or group prayers
leaders and hierarchy	announcers and acknowledgements	leaders and hierarchy	leaders and hierarchy
rules/ holy writings	Rule Book	Handbooks of conducts, rules & regulation	Handbooks of conducts, rules & regulation
rituals	The Wave, clapping, cheering		
superstitions, relics, charms	superstitions, relics, charms	merit badges	medal, honors and awards
markings and painting of body	markings and painting of body	******	markings and painting of body
Historical importance	Statistics to no end	Historical importance	Historical importance
Idols	Idolization of famous	******	******
faith	faith	community	commaradarie
oppposition leading to killing	Riots, deaths	friendly competition	killing for the greater good
us vs. them mentality	us vs. them mentality	******	kill or be killed mentality
Sacrifice	Terms like sacrifice, battle	******	sacrifice for one's country
can apply for 501(c)3 tax exempt	can apply for 501(c)3 tax exempt	501(c)3 tax exempt	******

* Not all apsects are absolute. Some groups and sub-groups often have a wide range of application for any particular aspect. This table is quite general and meant only for open discussion.

References:

Statista. (2023, May 4). Sports fans share in the U.S. 2023.
https://www.statista.com/statistics/300148/interest-nfl-football-age-canada/

YPulse. (2023, June 15). NA vs WE: Who Are the Bigger Sports Fans? - YPulse.
https://www.ypulse.com/article/2022/05/19/we-na-vs-we-who-are-the-bigger-sports-fans/

Kottak, C. P. (2019). *Mirror for Humanity: A Concise Introduction to Cultural Anthropology*.

Peretz, E., & Fox, J. A. (2021). Religious Discrimination against Groups Perceived as Cults in Europe and the West. *Politics, Religion & Ideology*, volume *22, no.* 3-4, pages 415–435.
https://doi.org/10.1080/21567689.2021.1969921

Rough Initiations – Rites of Passage

Rough initiations is another term for rites of passage, which can be ceremonial events that mark important transitions in an individual's life. A rough initiation refers to the challenging aspects of an initiation process or symbolic ritual. These events often involve the change of one's social status, roles, or responsibilities within a family, group or community. Initiations are a common element within rites of passage, taking various forms or presentations.

Challenges may involve physical and/or psychological challenges of endurance, meant to push an individual to achieve their full potential, capacity or limits. By overcoming these challenges, the individual can demonstrate their willingness and qualifications to accept new roles or responsibilities within a particular group or community. Rough initiations are integral to various cultures and traditions around the world, where they are often designed specifically to assess an individual's strength, fortitude, courage, resilience, and loyalty to a group or community. Details and particulars for rough initiations vary widely, but most have the underlying purpose of facilitating personal growth, strengthening of social bonds, and promoting a sense of identity and worth within the group.

I don't think that our current American culture offers much in the way of positive reinforcement of any real "coming of age" initiations or rites of passage. Common American initiations over the years have typically been the introductions of smoking cigarettes, drinking of alcohol, driving our first automobile, graduation from high school, and religious ceremonies of confirmation, bar/bat mitzvahs and other initiations that usher the individual into adulthood. Some of these previous examples other than the religious ones, can on some level be loosely interpreted as Francis Weller defined initiation, as "a contained encounter with death." Upon further reading of Francis Weller's Rough Initiations, what first started to catch my attention is that not everyone experiences things in quite the same way. For what may be traumatic for one individual might be trivial or an inconvenience for another. My understanding of trauma beyond the actual definition of events that our done to someone mentally and physically that manifest suffering to the individual, is that trauma most often comes at us unwelcomed, unannounced and usually free of a monetary charge. Initiations (rough or otherwise) on the other hand, are often welcomed, announced well ahead of time, seen as acceptance into adulthood, and for some there may be a monetary reward or financial fee in order for the initiation to be held.

Trauma is firsthand experiences or witnessing of physical injury/violence, abusive/toxic environments, death of a loved one, etc. Modern day rough initiations might be seen in religious ceremonies, the first hunt/fishing, cold/hot plunge, an intense mountain hike, college all-nighter, fasting, isolation, sleep deprivation and other tests that may challenge someone to perform at higher levels of physical activity and mental discipline. Basically, trauma comes to us, whereas we may pursue rough initiations, or so I have come to understand. We are all quite literally wired differently in regard to our own physiological nervous system, that often helps us to interpret stimuli as either positive or negative to mental, physical, and spiritual well-being. I do think that other cultures, may still hold their initiations of upmost importance, as I have come to learn more about that of indigenous peoples throughout the world.

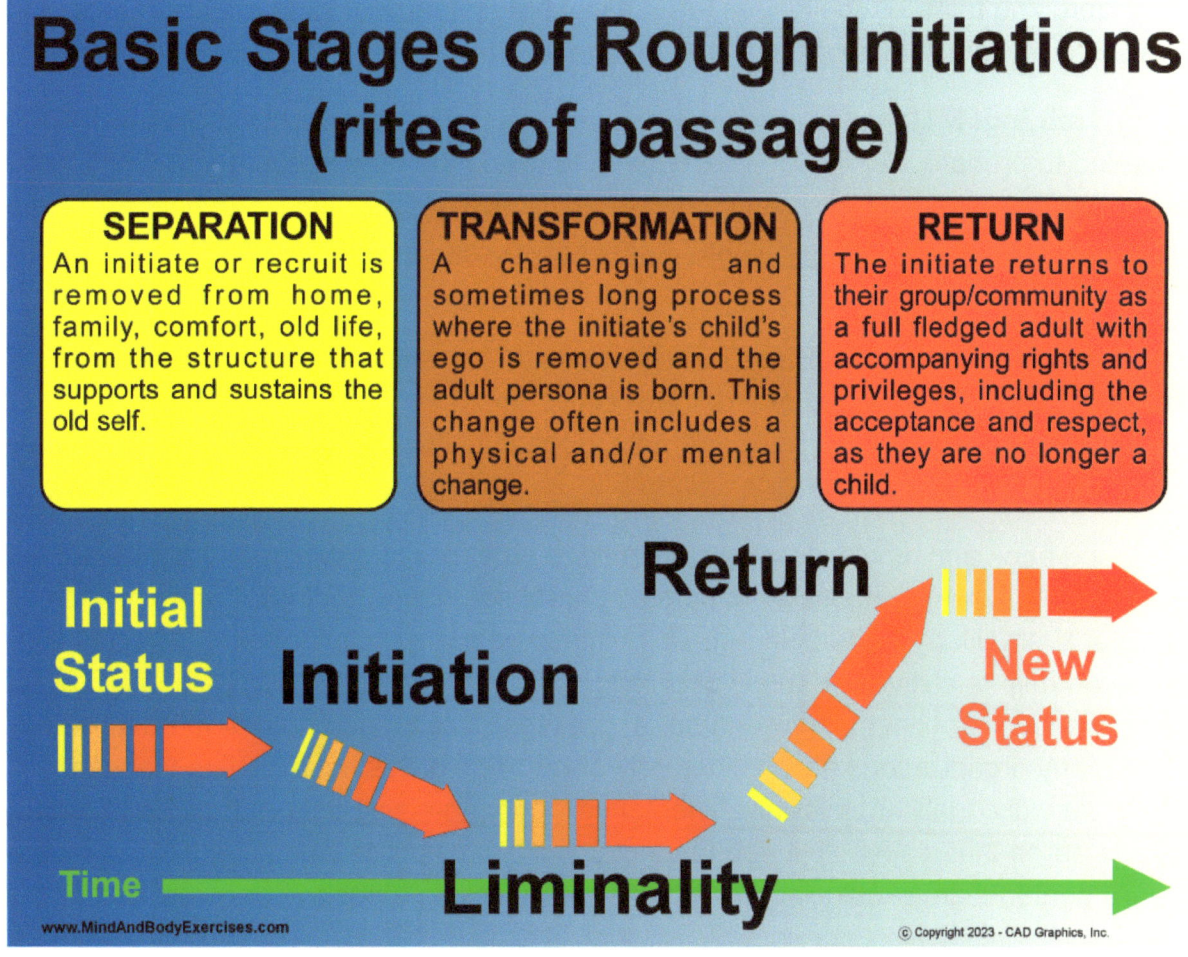

This is not a new concept as we can see examples from ancient times, where groups such as the Spartans, Romans, Vikings, Samurai, Mongols, the Knights Templar, Benedictines, Franciscans, Native Indigenous people worldwide, secret societies, and perhaps many others have had their own particular initiations and rites of passage. In more modern times, rough initiations can still be found in various presentations, although they may not be as common or standardized as some traditional cultural practices. Here are some examples:

Cultural or Social Initiations: Cultures, subcultures or social groups can have initiation rituals that require symbolic actions or engaging in challenging tasks that can range from endurance challenges to symbolic acts designed to demonstrate loyalty to the values of a group.

Fraternity/Sorority Hazing: Many organizations discourage, restrict and even ban hazing, however some fraternities and sororities still include initiation rituals that can be physically or emotionally challenging.

Sports Initiations: College and professional sports may have initiation rituals that involve rookies undergoing tasks or challenges, or participation in team-building events in order to demonstrate their commitment or loyalty to their team.

Military Training: Military basic training involves physically, and mentally challenging tasks needed to prepare recruits for the demanding risks they may encounter in their roles as soldiers. Initiation activities may include intense physical fitness routines, such as "hell week," and other psychological stress events that help to build discipline, resilience and camaraderie.

Specialized Training Programs: Elite military units, law enforcement agencies, first responder emergency teams and others may require their members to participate in stressful training which may be considered as extremely rough initiations, to ensure they are prepared for life and death situations.

Authors in the book and movie industry have played an enormous role in promoting this whole concept of rough initiations as can be seen in a seemingly endless stream of titles such as Star Wars, Harry Potter, Narnia, The Matrix and many, many others. Challenging initiations can help to cultivate a sense of belonging, camaraderie and commitment, however there is a nuanced relationship between beneficial rites of passage and detrimental hazing practices. Many organizations now deliberately discourage or restrict activities that can potentially put individuals at physical or mental risk, compromising their overall well-being. Most would agree that responsible and respectable initiative processes should focus on the individual's personal growth, social connections, and instilling a positive sense of belonging.

Iron Palm training (strategic trauma or rough initiations)

Reading Rough Initiations brought some memories back from my first years in my martial arts (cult)ure and having experienced many initiations. I refer to it as such because at this time of the early 1980's, American and Eastern cultures from China and Korea did not exactly assimilate well with each other in the conservative Midwest. One person's culture can very well be seen as another's cult. This can be quite apparent as seen today regarding one's religious, philosophical, and sometimes political beliefs. Even facets in pop culture, social issues and sports can reflect this divide between perspectives of what trends seem to have their own culture. With the former being said, the martial arts community of years past was often viewed as having its own unique culture as demonstrated in its traditions, rituals, and ceremonies.

My lineage did indeed focus beyond the basic goal of self-defense, due to the deep Taoist and Buddhist roots of my teachers. I was not quite aware of this before my first introductions, but I would soon learn that most martial arts systems are indeed rooted in having a series of initiations or tests, designed to bring an individual at least from being physically and mentally weak to that of enhanced physical and mental strength, and for those interested in cultivating higher spiritual awareness. I too have sought out rough initiations or "voluntary suffering" in what I would later learn to be called strategic trauma. Intense exercise, meditation, fasting, sensory deprivation, isolation and other methods of self-cultivation can be considered types of self-induced strategic trauma. "Iron palm" training is one such method of self-induced trauma that I did willfully partake in. Mental, physical and self-awareness benefits can be achieved from skillfully hitting bags of dried beans and then applying medicinal herbs and acupressure techniques thereafter to promote healing.

I think when others recognize an individual for having accepted these challenges either on their own volition or with the guidance, encouragement, and assistance from others, these events are now transformed into initiations. We as a group, consisting of my teachers, peers, and later my students under my guidance, did heavily invest in Weller's five variables of initiations that are the same used to heal individual trauma. These variables are community, ritual, the sacred, time and place. These components can help stabilize and anchor our inner dialogue, when either coping with traumatic life-changing events or self-cultivation.

References:

Writings. (n.d.). Francis Weller. https://www.francisweller.net/writings.html

Hewitt, D. (2021, November 27). 18 Memorable Coming of Age Rituals from History. History Collection. https://historycollection.com/18-memorable-coming-of-age-rituals-from-history/

Ancient Paths, Modern Peace: The Many Names of Enlightenment

In today's evolving conversation around holistic health, enlightenment is resurfacing-not just as an esoteric ideal, but as a practical and deep personal milestone within the journey toward total well-being. While often associated with mystics and monks, the essence of enlightenment has long been embedded across spiritual and philosophical traditions. It speaks to a universal longing: to understand oneself and one's place in the world, to live with clarity, and to experience inner peace.

Holistic health recognizes that true wellness includes not only the body but also the mind and spirit. When we explore enlightenment through this lens, it becomes less about dogma and more about the integration of awareness, connection, and personal transformation.

The Ancient Roots of Enlightenment: A Chronological Perspective

Across time and culture, humanity has reached for a transcendent state of wisdom and peace. Below is a historical look at how various traditions have been understood and named this experience:

1. Hinduism (c. 1500-1200 BCE)
Moksha refers to liberation from the cycle of rebirth (*samsara*) and the realization of one's oneness with the Absolute (*Brahman*). It emphasizes self-discipline, devotion, and philosophical inquiry-principles that resonate with today's holistic approaches to mindfulness and self-mastery.

2. Judaism (c. 1200-1000 BCE)
Devekut means "cleaving to God." It reflects an intense spiritual attachment and connection to the Divine, often nurtured through prayer, meditation on sacred texts, and acts of compassion. This mirrors modern interests in sacred ritual and spiritual intimacy within daily life.

3. Taoism (c. 600-400 BCE)
Wu Wei, or "effortless action," describes harmony with the *Tao*, or the natural order of the universe. It aligns beautifully with holistic living that promotes flow, simplicity, and balance through nature-based rhythms and minimalism.

4. Buddhism (c. 500 BCE)
Nirvana is the extinguishing of suffering, ignorance, and attachment. It is the ultimate liberation, discovered through the practice of mindfulness, ethical living, and meditative insight. *Bodhi*, or awakening, describes the experiential realization that leads to this state.

5. Christianity (c. 30 CE)
Illumination refers to the inner light that arises from divine communion. Practices like contemplative prayer, solitude, and service are paths to this inner radiance-echoing today's focus on stillness, presence, and soul care.

6. Islam (Sufism) (7th century CE)
Fana means the annihilation of the ego in the presence of God. In Sufi mysticism, it represents a deep surrender to divine love and truth-concepts that are increasingly embraced in emotional healing and ego work in holistic circles.

7. Sikhism (15th century CE)
Mukti signifies liberation from illusion and ego, and union with the Divine. It emphasizes selfless service, devotion, and equality principles foundational to both spiritual growth and community wellness.

8. New Age & Contemporary Spirituality (20th century CE onward)
Awakening / Self-Realization are the modern synthesis of East and West view of enlightenment as awakening to one's true nature. It often includes energy healing, intuitive development, and psychological integration-key aspects of the modern wellness movement.

Enlightenment and Holistic Wellness Today
In the context of holistic health, enlightenment is not about escaping the world. It's about engaging more deeply with it-intentionally, mindfully, and compassionately. Whether it's through yoga, mindful breathing, journaling, plant-based living, or spiritual inquiry, modern seekers are finding meaning in small, integrative practices that support mental clarity, emotional balance, and spiritual peace.

Importantly, enlightenment today is rarely seen as a final destination. Instead, it is a living process-a series of ongoing realizations and subtle shifts in consciousness. As individuals become more aware of their thoughts, behaviors, and purpose, they naturally align with states once reserved for sages and saints.

Why This Matters

In a time marked by information overload, stress, and disconnection, the timeless quest for enlightenment reminds us to return to our core. Holistic health is not just about the absence of disease-it is about the presence of meaning, clarity, compassion, and connection. Enlightenment, in all its cultural forms, is a call back to wholeness.

Whether you name it nirvana, moksha, awakening, or simply inner peace, the pursuit of higher awareness remains one of humanity's most enduring and necessary journeys.

PART III: MYSTICISM & INTERNAL TRADITIONS

Understanding the Korean Lunisolar Calendar and Mystical Time Cycles

Introduction

In Chinese and Korean astrology and traditional cosmology, time is conceptualized as cyclical and governed by natural forces. These systems are used in *saju* analysis, geomancy, and ritual calendars. Two fundamental components of this worldview are:

1. The **10 Heavenly Stems** (*Tian Gan* - **Chinese**), *Cheon-gan* - **Korean**)
2. The **12 Earthly Branches** (*Di Zhi* – **Chinese**), (*Ji-ji* - **Korean**)

Together with the **Five Elements (*Wuxing*)** and **Yin - Yang duality**, they create a sexagenary (60-day) cycle that is the basis for identifying auspicious days and mapping personal fate (Lee, 1981).

Heavenly Stems – 天干 *tian gan*

1	2	3	4	5	6	7	8	9	10
Yang	Yin	Yang	Yin	Yang	Yin	Yang	Yin	Yang	Yin
Jia	Yi	Bing	Ding	Wu	Ji	Geng	Xin	Ren	Gui
甲	乙	丙	丁	戊	己	庚	辛	壬	癸
Wood	Wood	Fire	Fire	Earth	Earth	Metal	Metal	Water	Water

Earthly Branches – 地支 *di zhi*

I	II	III	IV	V	VI	VII	VIII	IX	X	XI	XII
Yang	Yin	Yang	Yin	Yang	Yin	Yang	Yin	Yang	Yin	Yang	Yin
Zi	Chou	Yin	Mao	Chen	Si	Wu	Wei	Shen	You	Xu	Hai
子	丑	寅	卯	辰	巳	午	未	申	酉	戌	亥
Water	Earth	Wood	Wood	Earth	Fire	Fire	Earth	Metal	Metal	Earth	Water
Rat	Ox	Tiger	Rabbit	Dragon	Snake	Horse	Goat	Monkey	Rooster	Dog	Pig

Part 1: The 10 Heavenly Stems (Cheon-gan)

The Heavenly Stems are a 10-day cycle derived from the Five Elements:

- **Wood (木)** – Spring
- **Fire (火)** – Summer
- **Earth (土)** – Transition

- **Metal (金)** – Autumn
- **Water (水)** – Winter

Each element has a *Yang* (active) and *Yin* (receptive) form, yielding 10 total stems (Yoon, 2017).

These stems are associated with cardinal directions and form the energetic "climate" of each day:

Korean version of the 10 Heavenly Stems (Cheon-gan)

Number	Stem	Element	Polarity	Direction
1	갑 (Gap)	Wood	Yang	East
2	을 (Eul)	Wood	Yin	East
3	병 (Byeong)	Fire	Yang	South
4	정 (Jeong)	Fire	Yin	South
5	무 (Mu)	Earth	Yang	Center
6	기 (Gi)	Earth	Yin	Center
7	경 (Gyeong)	Metal	Yang	West
8	신 (Sin)	Metal	Yin	West
9	임 (Im)	Water	Yang	North
10	계 (Gye)	Water	Yin	North

These rotating influences affect *feng shui*, health, and calendar-based rituals (Wu, 2005)

Part 2: The 12 Earthly Branches (Ji-ji)

The Earthly Branches create a 12-day cycle and are symbolized by the 12 zodiac animals. Each branch has corresponding elemental, directional, and seasonal meanings.

Korean version of the 12 Earthly Branches (*Di Zhi*)

Branch	Animal	Element	Direction
자 (Ja)	Rat	Water	North
축 (Chuk)	Ox	Earth	NNE
인 (In)	Tiger	Wood	NE
묘 (Myo)	Rabbit	Wood	East
진 (Jin)	Dragon	Earth	ESE
사 (Sa)	Snake	Fire	SE
오 (O)	Horse	Fire	South
미 (Mi)	Goat	Earth	SSW
신 (Sin)	Monkey	Metal	SW
유 (Yu)	Rooster	Metal	West
술 (Sul)	Dog	Earth	WNW
해 (Hae)	Pig	Water	NW

Each day of the lunar month has an assigned branch, and this is one way that daily energy is determined (Kim, 2018).

Part 3: The 60-Day Cycle (Yukship Gapja)

Because 10 and 12 have a least common multiple of 60, this pairing forms a cosmological sequence that completes once every 60 days or years, depending on the calendar scale (Lee, 1981).

This cycle underlies:

- Daily calendar rotation
- 60-year birthday celebrations
- Spiritual timing for rituals and divination

The 60 units are viewed as elementally distinct days, each with specific fortune or taboo status.

Part 4: Special Days in Korean Mystical Practice

1. Sonnal – Unlucky Days

Rather than being "auspicious," these are dangerous or unlucky days, often tied to folk shamanic beliefs. They are days when:

- One should not cut hair or nails
- Surgery or travel is discouraged
- Avoid beginning manual tasks with construction, cutting, repairs, etc.
- Spirit intrusion is considered high (Kim, 2018)

2. Gil-il – Lucky Days

These are selected based on:

- Stem–branch harmony (Heavenly Stem supports the Earthly Branch)
- Lack of elemental conflict with the person's *saju* chart
- Favorable directional flow based on geomantic readings (Yoon, 2017)

In rural traditions, agricultural festivals or ancestral rites are often aligned with these dates. These are perceived as the best days for weddings, moving into a house, starting businesses, making kimchi, conceiving a child.

3. December as Auspicious?

There is some belief that the lunar month aligned with **Rat (Ja-wol),** roughly December in the Gregorian calendar is energetically potent, because:

- It is the start of the solar calendar (dongji, or winter solstice, marks the return of yang energy)
- It represents fertility and rebirth in seasonal logic (Wu, 2005)

However, no universal doctrine marks December as always auspicious; it depends on the year's alignment and individual energy patterns.

Part 5: Application in Korean Spiritual Life

- **Saju-palja**: Four Pillars of Destiny combines year, month, day, and hour to forecast character, fate, and life timing. Each pillar has a stem–branch combination.
- **Pungsu-jiri**: Korean geomancy uses directional alignments of time and space based on these cycles, to site homes, graves, and sacred spaces (Yoon, 2017).
- **Almanac Use**: Traditional Korean almanacs list each day's stem–branch, auspicious tasks, and prohibitions.

Conclusion

The purpose of this article is not to judge or critique these particular belief systems but rather offer information on differing perspectives. The integration of Heavenly Stems, Earthly Branches, Five Elements, and Yin-Yang philosophy produces a deeply symbolic and cyclical framework for interpreting time in Korean mysticism. Whether identifying auspicious dates, planning ancestral rites, or decoding one's destiny, these systems offer a structured metaphysical map of existence. Understanding them opens a window into a worldview where time, space, and spirit are intimately connected.

References:

Heavenly stems and earthly branches. (n.d.).
https://www.hko.gov.hk/en/gts/time/stemsandbranches.htm?utm_source=chatgpt.com

Kim, C. (2018). Korean shamanism. In Routledge eBooks. https://doi.org/10.4324/9781315198156

Lee, J. Y. (1981). Korean Shamanistic rituals. In Leo Laeyendecker & Jacques Waardenburg (Eds.), *Religion and Society* (Vol. 12). Mouton Publishers. https://api.pageplace.de/preview/DT0400.9783110811377_A33483020/preview-9783110811377_A33483020.pdf?utm_source=chatgpt.com

Yoon, H. (Ed.). (2017). P'ungsu: A Study of Geomancy in Korea. State University of New York Press. https://doi.org/10.2307/jj.18254509

Wu, S. (2005). *Chinese Astrology: Exploring the Eastern Zodiac*. Tuttle Publishing. https://archive.org/details/chineseastrology0000wush

Korean Neigong: Internal Cultivation Systems

Korean *neigong*, or internal cultivation, represents a rich and multifaceted tradition rooted in the intersections of *Seon (Zen) Buddhism, Daoism*, indigenous shamanism (*Muism*), and martial arts. Though often compared to Chinese *neidan* (internal alchemy), Korean systems possess their own unique methods, spiritual philosophies, and training structures. These practices cultivate internal strength, breath control, meditative awareness, and according to lineage traditions, can even develop extraordinary energetic capabilities within the human body.

Foundations of Korean Internal Cultivation

At the core of Korean *neigong* is the concept of *danjeon* training, the Korean analog to the Chinese *dantian*, representing energy reservoirs in the lower abdomen, heart center, and forehead. Training typically begins with breath regulation (*hoheupbeop*), emphasizing deep abdominal breathing and the storage of *gi* (*qi*), in the lower *danjeon*. Complementary postural training fosters rootedness and structural alignment to optimize energetic circulation.

Breathing practices are often paired with dynamic postures (*dong gong*) and stillness meditation (*jing gong*). Stillness can take the form of seated meditation (*jwaseon*), standing meditation (*ipseon*), or lying meditation (*woseon*). These practices are further enhanced by internal visualizations and energy circuit training (e.g., small celestial circulation (*so cheon-ju*), echoing the microcosmic orbit known in Daoist internal work.

Ethical cultivation is not separated from physical training. In Seon Buddhism, self-discipline, clarity of mind, and non-attachment are prerequisites for deeper spiritual realization. Korean shamanism and folk practices also include cathartic or vibrational techniques intended to release emotional and energetic blockages (Kendall, 2009).

Energy Centers of the Human Body

www.MindandBodyExercises.com

Different schools of thought exist as to how energy exists within and around the human body. This guide presents a summary for some of these theories as well as other naturally occurring phenomena within the human mind, body and spirit. These concepts seem new to Western culture, although other cultures have accepted their existence at least for many generations if not, thousands of years.

The Aura

Is the energy produced by your life force, and it radiates all around you. Similar to a radio antenna, the aura can receive or broadcast positive or negative energy from an individual. Your mental, emotional and physical state is reflected in your aura. The aura is constantly changing in color, shape and size. The strength and integrity of your aura will have a strong effect on your overall well being.

Chakras

Coming from traditional Indian medicine, there exist 7 energy centers within the human body. These points are considered the focal points for the reception and transmission of energies. Some believe believe the chakras interact with the body's ductless endocrine glands and lymphatic system by feeding in positive energies and disposing of unwanted negative energies. Each chakra in your spinal column is believed to influence or direct bodily functions near its region of the spine.

Dan Tiens

There are 3 Dan Tien, or energy centers within the human body. The upper Dan Tien is located between the eyebrows and is associated with higher awareness. The middle Dan Tien is located near the center of the chest and effects he immune system by stimulating the heart and lungs. The lower Dan Tien is located just below the naval and effects the storage of energy in the kidneys.

Energy Meridians

There are 12 main medians and 8 other special meridians within the human body. Meridians are similar to electrical wires or nerves. They run from the top of the head to the tips of the toes and finger. Each meridian is associated with an internal organ. When there is a lack of flow or blockage within the meridians, health problems can arise. Through proper diet, exercises and life style, it is possible to keep the chi flowing through the meridians.

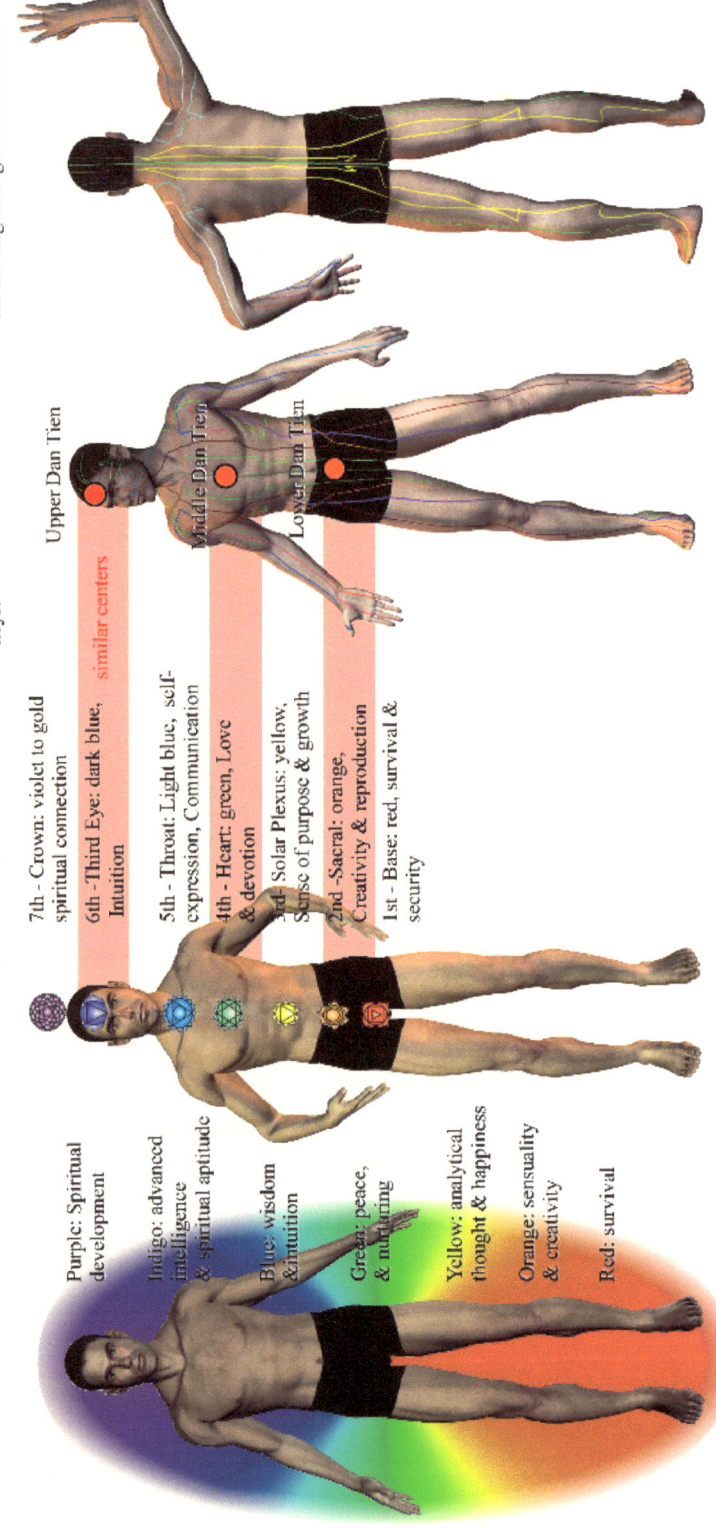

Purple: Spiritual development

Indigo: advanced intelligence & spiritual aptitude

Blue: wisdom & intuition

Green: peace, & nurturing

Yellow: analytical thought & happiness

Orange: sensuality & creativity

Red: survival

7th - Crown: violet to gold spiritual connection

6th - Third Eye: dark blue, Intuition

5th - Throat: Light blue, self-expression, Communication

4th - Heart: green, Love & devotion

3rd - Solar Plexus: yellow, Sense of purpose & growth

2nd - Sacral: orange, Creativity & reproduction

1st - Base: red, survival & security

similar centers

Upper Dan Tien

Middle Dan Tien

Lower Dan Tien

NOTE: This study guide is a general reference for the concepts shown.

© Copyright 2016 - CAD Graphics, Inc.

I. Core Practices in Korean Neigong

1. Breathing Techniques

- Emphasis on abdominal breathing focused on the *danjeon*, Korea's equivalent to *dantian*
- Breath retention and pressurization techniques to build internal heat and energy

2. Danjeon Development

- Training begins with the lower danjeon as the energy reservoir, with advanced practice involving the middle and upper danjeon
- Strengthening of energy through posture, breath, and mental focus

3. Stillness & Movement Forms

- Alternation between static meditation (*jing gong*) and dynamic exercises (*dong gong*)
- Includes seated (*jwaseon*), standing (*ipseon*), and walking meditations (Wŏnhyo. (2007)

4. Energy Circulation Pathways

- Refinement of energy through microcosmic and macrocosmic orbit-like methods
- Known in Korean as *So Cheon-ju* and *Dae Cheon-ju*, reflecting small and great celestial circuits

5. Vocal Resonance and Chanting

- Use of sound (vibration or mantra) to stimulate meridians or brain centers
- Buddhist *hwadu* practice or shamanic incantations are used for energetic activation (Kendall, 2009)

6. Moral and Spiritual Development

- Cultivation of *shin* (spirit) and refinement of *ki* (qi) is inseparable from ethical living, compassion, and clarity of mind
- These echo the Confucian and Buddhist emphasis on inner purity (Wŏnhyo. (2007)

II. Stages of Progression in Neigong

Korean systems typically follow a three-phase transformation of internal substances, paralleling Daoist inner alchemy:

Stage	Focus	Goal
1. **Jeong**	Essence	Cultivation and storage in lower danjeon
2. **Ki**	Energy	Circulation through meridians, activation
3. **Shin**	Spirit	Enlightenment, calm, and intuitive awareness

This structure reflects a philosophical progression from form to formlessness, body to spirit, and effort to naturalness (*mu-shim*).

III. Structured Systems in Lineage-Based Curricula

While historical documentation of standardized curricula is limited, several lineage-based or temple-administered systems reveal structured sequences of internal exercises.

1. Sunmudo

Sunmudo, a Korean Zen martial art maintained at *Golgulsa* Temple, exemplifies a synthesis of Seon meditation, martial forms, and yogic movement. Training includes:

- Breathing forms for energy refinement
- Dynamic martial sequences for vitality and physical strength
- Sitting meditation to deepen spiritual awareness

While specific counts of exercises vary, temple curricula often include dozens to hundreds of postures practiced cyclically and ceremonially (Gatling & Svinth, 2010; Buswell, 1992).

2. Sundo (Kouk Sun Do)

Sundo is a Daoist-based system emphasizing long-term energetic development through structured, belt-ranked progressions:

- Early stages introduce forms of 20–30 postures each, integrating breath and motion
- Intermediate levels include multiple 10–12 posture forms with increased internal pressure
- Higher ranks culminate in single postural meditations held for long durations

Though no canonical source confirms the existence of 640 exercises, advanced Sundo practitioners speak of multiple series comprising dozens of unique sequences, many kept orally or within private manuals (Baker, 2008).

3. Private and Temple-Based Neigong Curricula

Certain modern Daoist-influenced schools teach internal cultivation through sequential stages such as:

1. Ming Jin – Obvious or external power
2. An Jin – Hidden or internalized power
3. Hua Jin – Transformative or refined power

Each stage includes multiple breathing patterns, static postures, shaking or loosening exercises, and visualization practices. While primarily documented in Chinese systems, some Korean offshoots follow similar developmental arcs (DaoistMagic.com, 2018).

IV. The 640 Neigong Foundation Exercises

The **"640 foundational exercises"** for neigong training is an intriguing concept. While there seems to be no standardized system in Korea or China universally recognized by that number, similar structured sets have been mentioned in some martial and internal arts traditions.

Possible explanations:

1. **Categorized Curricula**: Some advanced traditional *neigong* systems (especially temple-based or private transmission lineages) are reported to have hundreds of discrete exercises, including:
   - Static postures (standing, seated)
   - Dynamic movements

- Meridian tapping or shaking
- Breath-retention patterns
- Visualizations or inner orbits

2. **Numerical Symbolism**: The number **640** may also be symbolic or organizational, reflecting a highly structured internal system for advanced practitioners. Comparable systems:
   - 72 movements in *Sundo*
   - 108 prostrations in Seon Buddhism
   - 360 meridian-related points, often doubled for bilateral flow

3. **Private or Temple Transmission**: It's plausible that a master or temple in Korea (or China) compiled a curriculum totaling 640 methods as part of a closed-door (*munpa*) tradition, though no academic or published source verifies this number explicitly.

V. Reports of Extraordinary Abilities and Energy Mastery

Anecdotal reports from both Korean and Chinese internal arts describe practitioners capable of moving energy to specific areas of the body at will, producing heat, shaking, or subtle vibration. Some traditions describe this as "naegong hwa" (internal fire) or "danjeon activation."

In *neijia* (internal martial arts) circles, Chinese masters have demonstrated:

- Fa jin – Explosive internal force from still postures
- Intentional energy projection through limbs or meridians
- Energetic sensitivity during partner work, reflecting advanced internal perception

While these claims lack robust scientific verification, ethnographic accounts support that dedicated practice over years may result in unusually fine motor control, breath retention capacity, and subjective energetic awareness (Buswell, 1992; ResearchGate, 2021).

In Korean contexts, practitioners of Sunmudo and Sundo have similarly reported the ability to move internal energy in ways that affect circulation, body temperature, or mental state. These effects are typically cultivated over decades of intensive, daily practice in monastic or semi-monastic settings. However, it is important to address, that "extraordinary claims, require extraordinary evidence," where a claim that is highly improbable or contradicts established knowledge, one should demand a higher standard of proof than for more ordinary claims. This principle, popularized by Carl Sagan, emphasizes that the strength of evidence needed to support a claim should be proportional to its degree of unusualness.

VI. Conclusion

Korean *neigong* is a dynamic and integrated tradition combining physical health, meditative stability, and moral clarity. Its practices span breath regulation, posture, mental focus, and internal energy movement, often embedded within temple or lineage-based systems.

While the concept of 640 foundational exercises remains unverified in published literature, structured multi-stage curricula in Sunmudo, Sundo, and other private lineages offer clear evidence of comprehensive internal development systems. Stories of energetic control or internal transformation continue to circulate in traditional circles, pointing to the long-term potential of dedicated inner practice, not necessarily as supernatural, but as refined physiological, neurological, and spiritual discipline.

Qigong & Neigong

- Qigong is a contemporary terminology, which got popular since the 60's of the last century. In the past, it was not called Qigong.

- QiGong is the energy skills for different purposes, e.g. health, martial arts, demonstration...

- Neigong refers to any of a set of Chinese breathing (Qi), body patterns (Form), stretching, and spiritual practice disciplines (Mind-intention, meditation) associated with *Daoism* and the *Chinese martial arts*

 ≠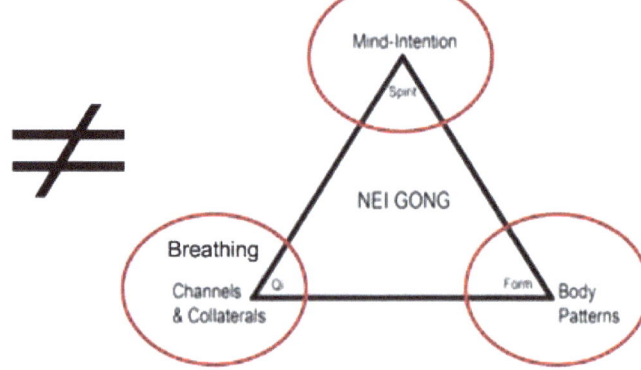

The Small or Microcosmic Circulation

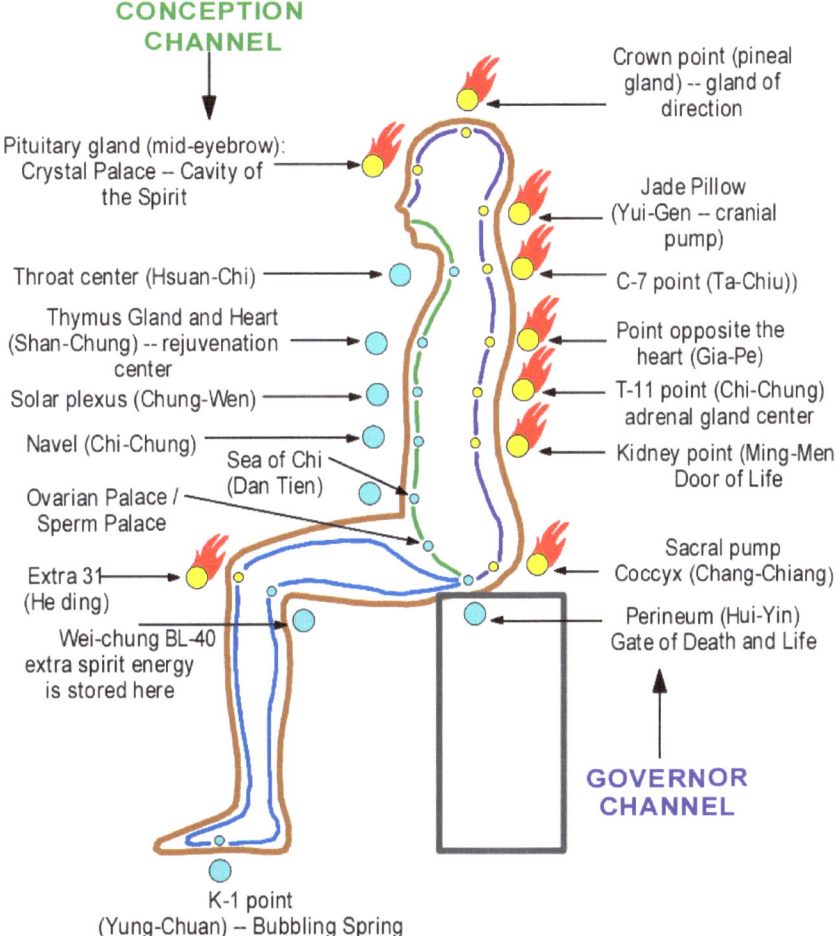

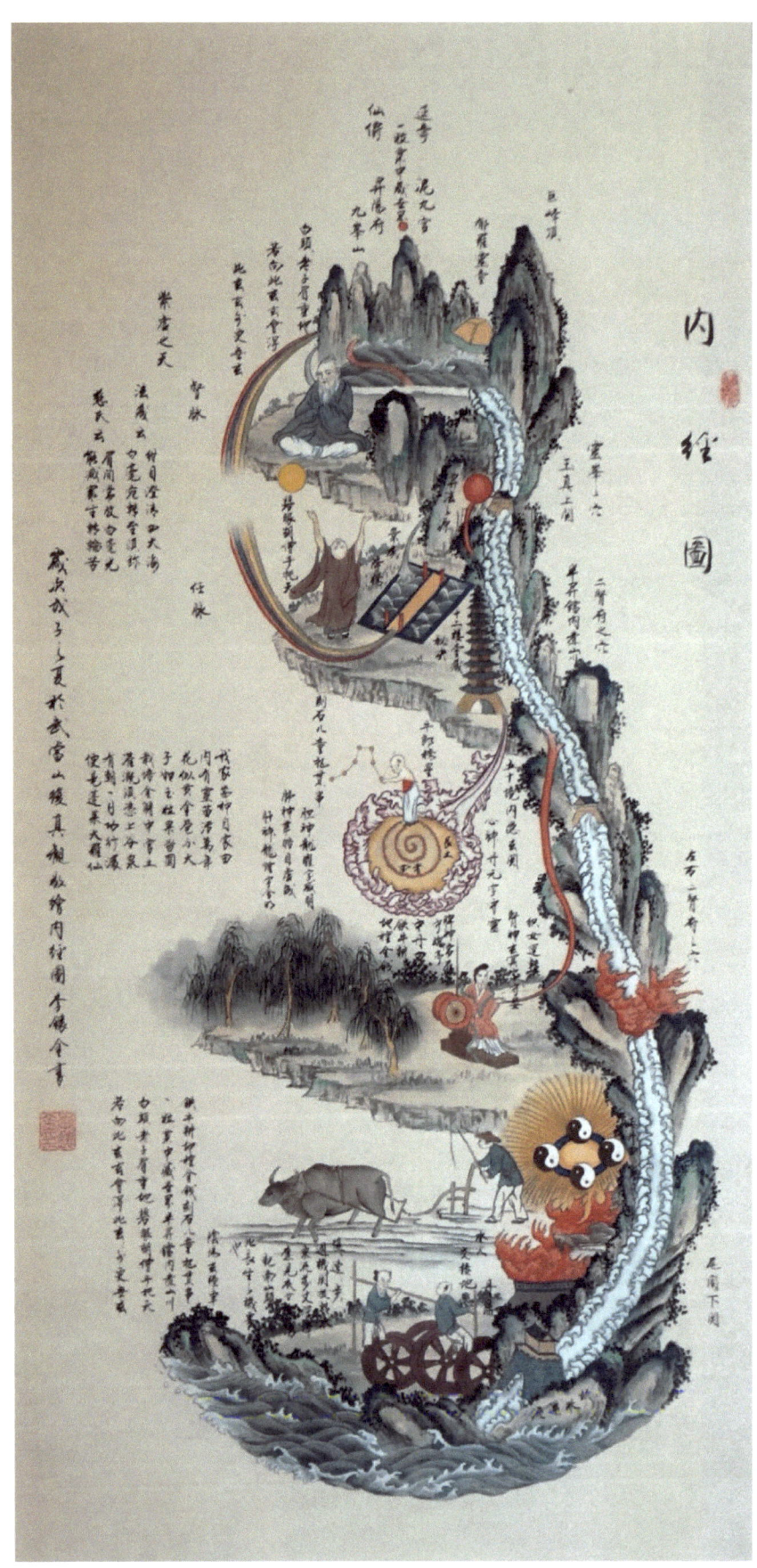

References:

Baker, D. L. (2008). *Korean Spirituality*. University of Hawaiʻi Press.
https://uhpress.hawaii.edu/title/korean-spirituality/

Buswell, R. E., Jr. (1992). *The Zen Monastic Experience: Buddhist Practice in Contemporary Korea*. Princeton University Press.
https://press.princeton.edu/books/paperback/9780691034775/the-zen-monastic-experience

DaoistMagic.com. (2018). *Neigong Training Curriculum Overview*. Retrieved July 2025, from https://www.daoistmagic.com/neigong-training-class

Kendall, L. (2009). *Shamans, Nostalgias, and the IMF: South Korean Popular Religion in Motion*. University of Hawaiʻi Press. https://archive.org/details/shamansnostalgia0000kend

Gatling, L., & Svinth, J. (2010). Martial arts of the world: An Encyclopedia of History and innovation. *www.academia.edu*.
https://www.academia.edu/3159277/Martial_arts_of_the_world_An_Encyclopedia_of_History_and_innovation

ResearchGate. (2021). *Hang the Flesh off the Bones: Cultivating an Ideal Body in Taijiquan and Neigong*. Retrieved from https://www.researchgate.net/publication/351059664

Wŏnhyo. (2007). Cultivating original enlightenment : Wŏnhyo's Exposition of the vajrasamādhi-sūtra (Paperback edition). University of Hawaiʻi Press.
https://searchworks.stanford.edu/view/13457065

Exploring Wei Dan, Qigong, and Nei Dan

A Detailed Summary to Daoist Alchemy from Chinese and Korean Internal Arts

Traditional Chinese internal arts offer a rich system of physical, energetic, and spiritual practices. Key concepts include **Wei Dan** (外丹), **Qigong** (气功), and **Nei Dan** (內丹). Understanding these three terms alongside their Korean martial arts parallels, clarifies important distinctions in the pursuit of health, self-mastery, and spiritual growth.

Wei Dan (外丹) – External Alchemy

Definition: "Outer Elixir." Wei Dan refers to ancient Daoist alchemical practices that sought to create physical elixirs for longevity or immortality by processing minerals and herbs externally (Pregadio, 2018).

Methods: Involves chemical experimentation with substances like mercury, arsenic, and cinnabar, (often highly toxic) which were ingested or used topically in pursuit of physical immortality.

Goals: Attain longevity or immortality by altering the body through external means.

Philosophy: Belief that the secrets of life and transformation can be discovered and harnessed in the material world outside the practitioner, reflecting an outward search for transcendence.

Qigong (气功) – Energy Skill

Definition: *"Energy Work."* Qigong encompasses practices that combine breath control, movement, visualization, and meditation to regulate and cultivate *qi*, the vital energy believed to animate life (Jahnke, 2002).

Method: Includes dynamic routines (e.g., Ba Duan Jin), static postures (e.g., Zhan Zhuang), breath regulation, and mental focus to circulate qi along the body's meridians.

Goals: Promote health, increase vitality, balance emotions, and prepare body and mind for advanced practices.

Philosophy: The human body is a microcosm of the universe, and by harmonizing breath, movement, and mind, practitioners align themselves with natural laws (Yang, 1997).

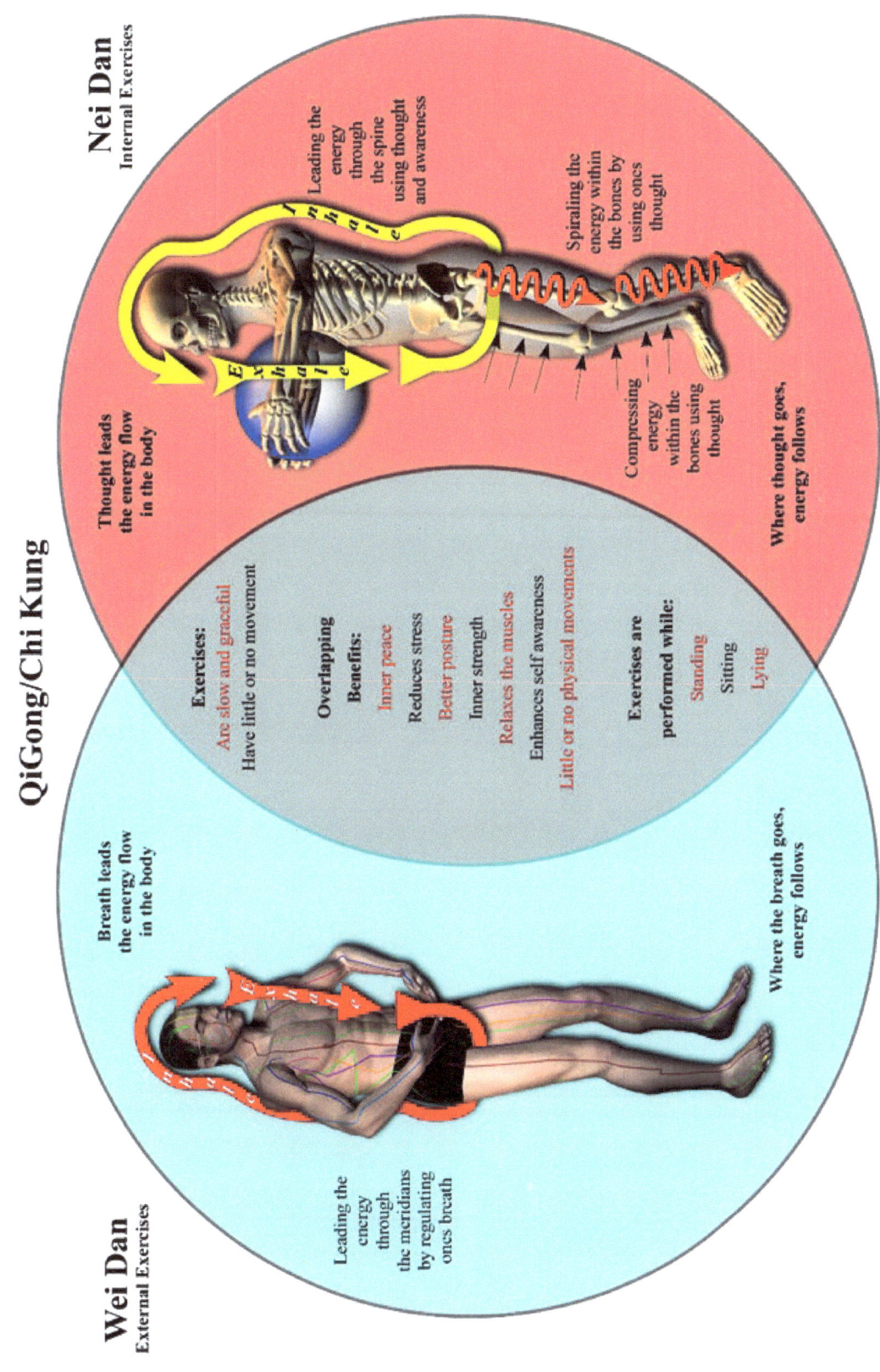

Nei Dan (內丹) – Internal Alchemy

Definition: *"Inner Elixir."* Nei Dan is the highest level of Daoist internal cultivation, dedicated to refining one's essence (jing), energy (qi), and spirit (shen) through advanced meditative and energetic practices (Mitchell, 2011).

Method: Involves breath retention, microcosmic orbit meditation, sexual energy control, visualization of energy flows, and progressive transformation of jing → qi → shen → emptiness (xu).

Goals: Achieve spiritual immortality, realization of one's true nature, and union with the Dao.

Philosophy: Transformation must occur internally; by purifying one's own mind-body-spirit, practitioners embody the Daoist ideal of returning to original emptiness and harmony with the cosmos.

Comparing Chinese and Korean Terms

Korean martial arts use similar-sounding terms of **Wae Gong, Gi Gong**, and **Nae Gong**, which overlap but don't always match the Chinese Daoist meanings:

Korean Term	Hangul / Hanja	Similar Chinese Concept	Same Practice?	Notes
Wae Gong	외공 / 外功	Wei Dan (外丹)	No	Refers to physical conditioning in martial arts, not Wei Dan's alchemy
Gi Gong	기공 / 氣功	Qigong 气功	Yes	Practices are nearly identical; focuses on breath, energy, and movement
Nae Gong	내공 / 內功	Nei Dan 內功	Partially	Internal energy work similar to Nei Gong; not necessarily advanced Nei Dan alchemy (Yang, 2007).

Etymological Breakdown of Chinese Characters

Understanding the roots of the Chinese characters deepens appreciation of these arts:

- 外 (Wài): 6 strokes. Components 夕 (*evening*) + 卜 (*divination*) → symbolizes seeking knowledge outside oneself.
- 气 (Qì): 4 strokes. Ancient forms depict swirling vapor → breath, vital energy.
- 內 (Nèi): 4 strokes. 冂 (*enclosure*) + 人 (*person*) → shows a person inside boundaries → introspection.

These etymologies reflect core Daoist themes of balancing inside (內) and outside (外), and cultivating qi (气) to align with the Dao (Qiu, 2000).

Integrated Comparison Table

Aspect	Wei Dan (外丹)	Qigong (气功)	Nei Dan (内丹)
Meaning	External elixir/alchemy	Energy skill/cultivation	Internal elixir/alchemy
Method	Chemical concoctions	Breath, movement, meditation	Advanced meditative transformation
Goal	Physical immortality	Health, vitality, stress relief	Spiritual immortality/enlightenment
Korean Parallel	Wae Gong (not equivalent)	Gi Gong (equivalent)	Nae Gong (partially equivalent)

Conclusion

Wei Dan, Qigong, and Nei Dan represent distinct layers of Daoist health and spiritual practices: Wei Dan's external focus, Qigong's energy cultivation, and Nei Dan's profound internal alchemy. Meanwhile, Korean martial arts terms like Wae Gong, Gi Gong, and Nae Gong reflect overlapping ideas but emphasize martial conditioning, energy work, and internal strength, respectively.

Understanding these differences empowers practitioners to choose a path aligned with their goals, whether health, martial skill, or spiritual awakening.

References:

Jahnke, R. (2002). *The Healing Promise of Qi: Creating Extraordinary Wellness Through Qigong and Tai Chi*. Contemporary Books.

Mitchell, D. (2011). *Daoist Nei Gong: The Philosophical Art of Internal Alchemy*. Singing Dragon

Pregadio, F. (2018). *The Taoist Alchemy: Nei Dan and Wei Dan in Chinese Tradition*. Golden Elixir Press.

Qiu, X. (2000). *Chinese Writing*. The Society for the Study of Early China & The Institute of East Asian Studies.

Yang, J. M. (2007). *Qigong for Health & Martial Arts: Exercises & Meditation*. YMAA Publication Center.

Note: I could find no single authoritative English-language source compiling the terminology of Wae Gong, Gi Gong, and Nae Gong. These terms are part of Korean martial arts oral traditions and school teachings, with meanings overlapping but not identical to the Chinese concepts discussed here.

Exploring the Thin Line Between Martial Legend and Human Potential

Across cultures and centuries, legends of warriors moving so swiftly they appear to multiply or vanish, have captivated imaginations. In Korean and Chinese martial lore, tales of masters performing techniques like *Kyung Gong Sul Bope* (light body skill) or the enigmatic *Sam Shim U Gye* describe practitioners moving so quickly or unpredictably that they seem to split into several forms. Similarly, certain Australian Aboriginal traditions tell of "shadow walking" or "mist walking," where skilled individuals could move in ways that made them appear as multiple figures or become nearly invisible to those pursuing them. These stories share a common thread: extraordinary mastery of timing, movement, and the environment, combined with a keen understanding of human perception.

Years back, I witnessed a live performance of Shaolin monks demonstrating extraordinary feats of physical strength as well as a level of self-discipline that I have never seen before. On another occasion, I attended a Bull's basketball game where Michael Jordan on numerous plays demonstrated his seemingly unique ability to walk on the air beneath him. These are examples of real people demonstrating extraordinary abilities. The late Bill Moyers, a renowned and respected journalist, composed a five-part television series (*Healing and the Mind*, 1993) where he investigated and reported his findings on Traditional Chinese Medicine and the concept of qi. Moyers was quite surprised at the efficacy of TCM in spite of his initial skepticism (Moyers, 1993).

Martial Arts Legends of Walking on Air

Kyung Gong Sul Bope (Korean), equivalent to the Chinese *Qing Gong*, is more clearly represented in martial records. These techniques developed from agility training involving explosive jumping, low stances, and breath control, often practiced by monks or guards (Shahar, 2008). The goal was not supernatural flight but increased speed, evasiveness, and physical control. There are some interesting demonstrations available online at:
https://www.youtube.com/watch?v=Obx6zXADsVQ,
https://www.youtube.com/watch?v=1GKwlfVCD2M,
https://www.youtube.com/watch?v=hGtrZKir7sY

Martial Arts Legends of Multiplicity

In Daoist literature and Chinese mythology, the concept of *fenshen*, meaning "dividing the body," is found in classical texts. For example, Ge Hong's *Baopuzi* (c. 320 CE) describes adepts capable of appearing in multiple places simultaneously. Similarly, Hui Jiao's *Memoirs of Eminent Monks* recounts stories of Buddhist practitioners performing multilocation or form-division feats (Hui Jiao, 1976). These accounts reflect a symbolic, ritualistic interpretation of spiritual multiplicity, rather than physical duplication.

In East Asian martial arts, the idea of *Sam Shim U Gye* is poorly documented but sometimes passed along in oral tradition. It is described as a principle allowing a practitioner to move so fast they seem to be in more than one place. Though not part of recognized martial literature, it echoes legends of shadow-splitting (*fen shen*) in Chinese folklore (Wikipedia, 2025).

The illusion of multiplicity arises from:

- Misdirection and broken rhythm
- Diagonal and lateral footwork
- Manipulation of the observer's focus and peripheral vision
- Exploitation of low-light conditions

While no martial artist has physically been proven to have multiplied themselves, highly trained practitioners can create confusion and overwhelm opponents through rapid, deceptive movements (Henning, 1999).

Aboriginal Shadow Walking

Among Australian Aboriginal groups, oral traditions describe "shadow walking" or "mist travel," where an individual may disappear into the landscape or appear to be more than one person. These stories, often rooted in Dreamtime cosmology, reflect actual survival and tracking expertise (Rose, 1992). Aboriginal trackers are renowned for nearly supernatural ability to read signs invisible to outsiders and move through terrain undetected.

Shadow walking includes:

- Mastery of terrain and environmental blending
- Controlled, timed movement
- Predictive awareness of pursuers' behavior
- Use of visual and auditory manipulation

These techniques are deeply practical, even if they appear mystical to outsiders (Chatwin, 1987).

Perception and Illusion: The Neuroscience

Human perception is imperfect, especially under stress. Several neurological and visual factors can explain illusions of multiplicity:

- **Persistence of vision**: brief visual impressions can linger, making movement appear blurred or doubled
- **Attentional blindness**: the brain struggles to register abrupt directional changes
- **Tunnel vision**: high-stress or fight-or-flight responses narrow focus

Such phenomena mean that highly skilled martial artists can exploit these perceptual gaps, creating the illusion of multiple attackers or vanishing movement.

Dim Mak: Myth, Medicine, and Martial Mystery

Another layer of martial myth surrounds *Dim Mak*, often called the "death touch." This practice, tied to *dian xue* (acupoint striking), claims that precise strikes to certain points can disable or kill. Stories extend to "delayed death," pressure paralysis, or even non-contact knockouts.

While Dim Mak is thematically linked to Traditional Chinese Medicine (TCM), its more mystical claims lack scientific support:

- Acupuncture points do not correspond with discrete anatomical structures (Langevin et al., 2001)
- Striking vital areas (e.g., carotid sinus, liver, solar plexus) can incapacitate, but this is anatomical vulnerability, not energetic disruption
- No-contact or delayed effects have failed empirical testing

Dim Mak demonstrations often rely on:

- Suggestibility and peer expectation (nocebo effect)
- Compliant students and dramatized reactions
- The absence of controlled or blinded trials

Such claims are best understood as cultural mythology rather than proven combat methodology (McCarthy, 1995).

Wuxia Cinema: Martial Fantasy on Film

Crouching Tiger, Hidden Dragon (2000) exemplifies the cinematic portrayal of these legends. As part of the *wuxia* tradition, the film depicts martial heroes performing:

- Light-body leaps and treetop duels, a visual extension of *qing gong*
- Acupressure-induced paralysis during combat
- Delayed death from poisoned needles

These elements, while fictional, reflect deeper cultural themes of spiritual cultivation and moral transcendence. Wuxia films stylize martial ability to express inner mastery and dramatic stakes (Shahar, 2008).

There are very talented and gifted people among us. However, if someone has been investing decades of their lives with the ambition of being able to jump from rooftop to rooftop, land safely from jumping off an eight-story building, or being able to project their inner vital force and have not achieved or come closer to obtaining these abilities, maybe it is time to reassess the difference between myth and reality. If your lineage or course of learning claims to teach extraordinary, supernatural or miraculous feats, it may be prudent to respectfully ask your teachers to demonstrate their claims. Proof in still photograph images from decades long past, do little to exude credibility in the here and now.

Modern Performance and Extraordinary Claims

In today's digital era, video footage showcases athletes, martial artists, and performers achieving astonishing feats. From Bruce Lee's lightning-fast punches to parkour practitioners scaling rooftops, we witness the real potential of human movement. These skills are remarkable but remain within the bounds of physics and biology.

As physicist Carl Sagan aptly stated, **"Extraordinary claims require extraordinary evidence"** (Deming, 2016). Martial arts traditions deserve respect for their transformative value, but supernatural interpretations must be held to the same standard of critical inquiry.

Conclusion

The legends of *Kyung Gong Sul Bope*, *Sam Shim U Gye*, *Dim Mak*, and Aboriginal shadow walking offer rich cultural insights into human potential, narrative tradition, and symbolic expression. While these phenomena are not supported by scientific evidence as literal realities, they reflect the enduring fascination with mastery, perception, and the boundaries of possibility.

Rather than diminishing these stories, understanding their metaphorical and psychological dimensions can deepen appreciation for the disciplines they arise from. In that light, they continue to inspire, challenge, and elevate the art of personal cultivation.

On a personal note, I have firsthand experience of various presentations of internal power (*qi* and/or *neidan, nei gong*) where I have felt an increase of warm vital energy through my own body. I have witnessed an individual be able to noticeably move internal energy and circulation to one arm, where their arm did become somewhat "puffy" compared to their other arm. I have seen and myself applied acupressure on numerous occasions, in specific sequences on others to both revive and incapacitate another person; first-aid and self-defense.

References:

Chatwin, B. (1987). *The Songlines*. Viking Press.

Chinese Myths 101. (2025, February 17). *Does Chinese Lightness Skill really exist? Qing Gong - Supernormal Abilities in Kung Fu* [Video]. YouTube. https://www.youtube.com/watch?v=1GKwlfVCD2M

Ge Hong. (trans. Ware, J. R.). (1966). *Alchemy, Medicine and Religion in the China of A.D. 320: The Nei Pien of Ko Hung*. Dover Publications.

Henning, S. E. (1999). Academia encounters the Chinese martial arts. *China Review International*, 6(2), 319–332. https://www.jstor.org/stable/23732172

Hui Jiao. (trans. Link, A.). (1976). *Lives of Eminent Monks*. Berkeley Buddhist Studies Series.

Langevin, H. M., Churchill, D. L., & Cipolla, M. J. (2001). Mechanical signaling through connective tissue: a mechanism for the therapeutic effect of acupuncture. *The FASEB Journal*, 15(12), 2275–2282. https://doi.org/10.1096/fj.01-0015hyp

Learn Chinese Now. (2024, July 22). *Supernormal abilities in Kung Fu - Lightness skill (Qing gong)* [Video]. YouTube. https://www.youtube.com/watch?v=Obx6zXADsVQ

McCarthy, P. (1995). *Bubishi: The classic manual of combat*. Tuttle Publishing.

Moyers, B. (1993). *Healing and the mind* [Television series]. Public Affairs Television.

Mr. Y Talks. (2023, July 22). *Unveiling the mysteries of Qing gong: the Gravity-Defying skill of Chinese kung fu* [Video]. YouTube. https://www.youtube.com/watch?v=hGtrZKir7sY

Rose, D. B. (1992). *Dingo makes us human: Life and land in an Australian Aboriginal culture*. Cambridge University Press.

Deming, David. (2016). Do Extraordinary Claims Require Extraordinary Evidence?. Philosophia. 44. 10.1007/s11406-016-9779-7.

Shahar, M. (2008). *The Shaolin Monastery: History, religion, and the Chinese martial arts*. University of Hawai'i Press.

Wikipedia contributors. (2025, June 9). *Fenshen*. Wikipedia. https://en.wikipedia.org/wiki/Fenshen

Feasibility and Legacy of Extensive Martial Arts Systems in the Modern Age

A Detailed Review of Long-Form Practices, Cognitive Limits, and Contemporary Application

With nearly 45 years of continuous study, practice, and teaching in the internal martial arts, I offer this article as both a practitioner and researcher deeply immersed in the tradition of **Baguazhang**. My experience spans several influential branches of the art, including *Sun, Cheng, Emei,* and *Chung* styles. Each has contributed to my understanding of the circular, spiraling, and dynamic principles that make Baguazhang a unique and profound martial system.

While I have not personally trained in **Qing Gong** (known in some Korean traditions as *Kyong Gong Sul Bope*), I have invested considerable time researching its historical claims, theoretical foundations, and relationship to internal martial development. My aim is not to present mystical exaggerations, but to critically examine the structure, feasibility, and legacy of extensive martial systems. In particular, those that claim hundreds of forms, internal skillsets, and unique training regimens.

This perspective is informed by decades of firsthand teaching experience, cross-style comparison, academic inquiry, and dialogue with both traditional lineage holders and modern researchers. The views presented here are grounded in practice, supported by analysis, and guided by a sincere respect for the martial arts as a lifelong path of cultivation.

Introduction

Throughout the world's martial traditions, extensive sequences of linked movements commonly referred to as **forms**, *kata, hyung, taolu,* or *jurus,* have been used as vehicles for transmitting fighting techniques, internal energy development, and philosophical insight. While some of these forms are brief and focused, others contain hundreds of techniques, and some practitioners claim that it may take 1 to 5 hours to complete in a single execution. This essay examines:

- The global context of long-form martial arts
- The feasibility of attaining proficiency in complex systems
- The practical application of such training in today's fast-paced world
- Whether it is realistic or even possible for one or a few individuals to retain and transmit massive bodies of knowledge like 640 foundational sets and 108 Bagua transitions
- And whether this model can thrive in modern martial arts culture

II. Global Martial Arts Traditions with Long-Form Practice

Numerous systems around the world preserve extended forms or sequences. These practices vary in complexity, purpose, and duration, but share the intention of transmitting depth of method and cultivating physical and internal mastery.

Chinese Martial Arts

- *Yang*-**style Taijiquan**: The traditional long form consists of **108 postures**, often practiced in **30–60 minutes**, or up to **2 hours** with slow breathwork.
- *Chen*-**style *Taiji Laojia Yilu***: A spiral-based internal form with **74–83 postures**, taking about **45–90 minutes**.
- *Shaolin Luohanquan*: Includes 18, 36, 72, or 108 movement forms, sometimes representing stages of internal/spiritual development.
- *Baguazhang*: Features **64 or 108 palm changes**, practiced with circle walking and flowing transitions, often extending practice well over **1–2 hours**.

Japanese Martial Arts

- **Karate Kata**: Systems like Shotokan include forms such as *Kanku Dai*, *Unsu*, or *Suparinpei*, each with dozens of transitions.
- Koryu Bujutsu: Ancient samurai traditions preserve long weapon kata or *omote*, *ura*, and *kumitachi*, each embedded with strategy and timing.
- **Aikido**: Though less formalized, Aikido includes long paired exercises with weapons like *jo* and *bokken*.

Korean Martial Arts

- **Taekwondo (Poomsae) / Tang Soo Do (Hyung)**: Structured sequences like *Tae guk* or *Pyong Ahn*, progressing in complexity and coordination.
- **Kuk Sool Won**: Incorporates striking, joint locks, acrobatics, and traditional weapon forms.

Indian and Southeast Asian Systems

- **Kalaripayattu**: Utilizes **meypayattu** (body flows) and **kalari vaittari** (commanded sequences) for strength and agility.
- **Silambam**: Weapon forms with long rhythmic staff patterns.
- **Pencak Silat**: Includes complex *jurus* and *langkah* systems.

Internal Cultivation & Daoist Systems

- *Yi Jin Jing / Xi Sui Jing:* Monastic routines of 49–100+ stages, possibly performed over **3+ hours**.
- **Neigong & Dao Yin**: Breath-driven meditative movement sets that stretch across 1 to 2-hour daily sessions.
- **Baguazhang Switching Drills**: 108 transitional palms (Top, Middle, Lower, with 36 each) used in continuous combat flow.

III. System Outline: Time and Structure

The following curriculum model is based on a traditional system studied directly by the author over decades of immersion. While not widely published, the methods are internally coherent and rooted in classic martial structure:

Training Duration Feasibility

Training Aspect	Duration	Feasibility Summary
Short Hyung (Dan Hyung)	5–35 minutes	✅ Very feasible with focused repetition. Excellent for limited-time sessions.
Middle Hyung (Joong Hyung)	10–45 minutes	✅ Highly feasible for modern practice. Allows depth, review, and memorization.
Long Hyung (Chang Hyung)	1.5–5 hours	⚠️ Feasible only in **segments**. Full-form execution is rare in modern life. Requires commitment and memory structuring.
Ship Pal Gae (18 Weapons)	30–90 minutes each	⚠️ Possible with **rotation and yearly focus** on 1–2 weapons at a time. Full mastery over a decade+ is realistic.
Wae Gong, Nae Gong, Kyong Gong Sul Bope (640 foundational sets)	Variable	⚠️ Theoretically possible but better approached **modularly**. Depth over breadth. Grouped by body type or principle.
Bagua Zhang Switching Drills (108)	1 sec per transition	✅ Very feasible. Develops into fluid combinations. Excellent daily integration into circle walking and form.

IV. BaguaZhang Switching Techniques (108 Foundational Switches)

BaguaZhang Palm Changes & 108 Switching Techniques

1. **General Principles & Training Methods**

- The "Eight Mother Palms" form the basis of Bagua internal development, practiced typically during circle walking. Each palm emphasizes body alignment, spiraling technique, and transitional mechanics (Chu, 2019).
- Expanded traditions (e.g., Yin or Gao styles) systematize palm changes into upper (top), middle, and lower transitions related to spiral alignment, kinetic linkages, and combat application

2. **Historical Context & Lineage**
   - Founder Dong Hai Chuan's students (Yin, Cheng, Gao lines) diversified the core palms into extensive sequences (e.g., 64-, 108-, or even 192-palm sets) (Chu, 2019).

3. **Practical Execution & Spiral Mechanics**
   - Palm change drills remain central to Bagua's characteristic evasive and spiral movements. They are practiced either as stand-alone drills or integrated into walking the circular pattern.

4. **Overview of Switching Techniques**
   - In *BaguaZhang* (8 trigram palm) "switching" refers to the palm change, which is the fundamental dynamic movement that allows a practitioner to alter direction, intent, angle, or application while walking the circle. These palm changes are typically modular, allowing them to be strung together like language.

   - Traditionally, Bagua styles such as **Sun, Cheng, Yin, Gao,** and **Liang** develop 8 core palm changes, which expand into multiple permutations and footwork variations. Advanced lineages (especially in Gao-style) systematize palm changes into **top (*Sung,* middle *(Jung)*, and lower *(Ha)* body initiations.

5. **Structure of 108 Switching Techniques**
   - **36 Top Switching Techniques (Sung)**
     - Initiated from the **upper body**: shoulders, arms, hands, and upper spine.
     - Often involve:
       - Overhead swings, downward palms, cloud hands
       - Strike deflections
       - Rotational arm/shoulder mechanics

- Head-level entries or wraps
    - These are closely tied to *Yang*-like motion: expansive, expressive, outward
- **36 Middle Switching Techniques (Jung)**
    - Centered on the **torso, hips, and waist**
    - Focus:
        - Spiral rotations from dantian
        - Mid-line redirections
        - Coiling waist motions to project energy
        - Interception and bridging techniques
    - Represent **transitional force**: the "change point" between top and bottom
- **36 Lower Switching Techniques (Ha 下)**
    - Originate from the **legs, footwork, stances, and dropping mechanics**
    - Include:
        - Sweeps, low kicks, stepping traps
        - Cross-stepping, deep pivots, root shifting
        - Defensive dodges from low angles
    - Tend to reflect *Yin*-like qualities: inward, sinking, redirective

6. **Integration into Practice**
- Switching techniques may be performed as:
    - **Standalone drills** (e.g., 5 switching drills per session)
    - **Embedded in circle walking routines**
    - **Linked into forms** or paired drills
- Many practitioners organize them seasonally (e.g., focusing on a layer for 3 months)
- Some styles break 108 into **3 series of 36**, which are further divided into **six 6-technique families**, often linked to elements or trigrams.

BaguaZhang (Pakua, moving meditation, circle walking)

www.MindandBodyExercises.com

8 Animal Characteristics   8 Fundamental Palms   8 Stepping Methods

Deep mindful breathing, specific muscle stretching and deliberate walking techniques are the basis of BaguaZhang exercises. Practicing BaguaZhang or Bagua, stepping positions, body postures and changes (transitional stretching movements) enables one to move your body like a spring, being flexible and light but having a lot of strength and power behind the movement. This would be similar to moving as light and smooth as a feather but having the strength and speed of a bear. Attaining certain body alignments within postures, holding that position and moving from one to another is essential to develop overall strength, coordination, balance and increase of energy flow throughout the body. Proper breathing is important in the development of internal strength and has to be in tune with each movement.

© Copyright 2018 - CAD Graphics, Inc.

V. Wae Gong, Nae Gong, Kyong Gong Sul Bope (640 Foundational Sets)

These three terms of **Wae Gong** (external power), **Nae Gong** (internal cultivation) (Wikipedia contributors, 2024), and **Kyong Gong Sul Bope** (aerial or mystical skill), represent progressive layers of skill development. The inclusion of **640 foundational sets**, divided by **8 hereditary types × 80 subsets**, supports a detailed, modular training system.

Qing Gong translates literally to "light skill" or "lightness technique." It refers to the ability to move the body lightly and rapidly, with agility and grace. While some Korean traditions refer to this as *Kyong Gong Sul Bope*, the broader and more recognized Chinese equivalent is Qing Gong, emphasizing aerial mobility, lightness, and rapid footwork to:

- Evade attacks
- Traverse difficult terrain
- Jump long distances or scale walls
- Appear to "float" or "glide"

Well-Documented Components

Component	Function	Modern Analog
Weighted step work	Builds leg power for jumping/landing	Plyometric training
Low stance work	Improves tendon recoil and gliding mobility	Isometric holds and tendon loading
Breath synchronization	Matches inhale/exhale to movement rhythm	Neigong, internal energy pacing
Climbing drills	Simulates wall-scaling, aerial coordination	Parkour, tactical wall-scaling drills

Each body type would ideally have **80 tailored micro-sets**, designed to:

- Compensation for biomechanical challenges
- Enhance strengths

- Reduce injury risk
- Maximize fluidity and function for that build

Each 80-set group may include drills or sequences from multiple domains. A **sample distribution** might look like:

Categories of the 80 Sets per Type

Category	# Sets	Example Focus
Wae Gong (External Power)	~30	Striking forms, structural alignment, repetition drills
Nae Gong (Internal Cultivation)	~20	Breath-body integration, dantian rotation, meditative form
Kyong Gong Sul Bope (Aerial/Light Skill)	~10	Leaping drills, evasions, sudden weight shifts
Conditioning & Recovery	~10	Joint prep, tendon strength, recovery movement
Specialized Drills (Hybrid)	~10	Blending categories, such as explosive internal transitions

Format of Each Set

Each "set" may be:

- A short form (30 sec to 2 minutes)
- A paired drill
- A static posture with breath regulation
- A moving neigong routine for soft-tissue engagement
- A dynamic jump/evasion/fall drill for Kyong Gong

These are not isolated movements but often sequential flows, comprising 5–12 linked actions, possibly with an internal theme or breathing rhythm.

Teaching and Rotation Strategy

Given the vast number of sets, a realistic teaching and retention method would require:

- Rotational cycles, focusing on 10–15 sets per quarter
- Tracking logbooks for both teacher and student
- Core sets used for all types (e.g., the "seed drills")
- Some sets exclusive to a body type (e.g., "Overweight" sets avoid deep stances early on)

VI. Training Frequency and Feasibility Over Time

✅ Ideal Scenario (1–2 hrs, 5–6 days/wk)

- Entire system could be internalized over **20–30 years**
- Structured cycles (e.g., seasonally rotating weapon or form focus)
- Internal cultivation and external technique blended over time

⚠️ Modern Constraints (1 hr, 3–4 days/wk)

- Prioritize core sets over totality
- Short and middle hyung are realistic anchors
- Bagua transitions and foundation sets can be explored in small segments
- Weapon work limited to 2–3 tools over 5–10 years

Best Practices

- **Modular training**: Break long forms into repeatable segments
- **Cyclic review**: Return to previously learned sets on a schedule
- **Specialization**: Focus on the sets or weapons that resonate with your goals or body constitution
- **Documentation**: Journaling and visual diagrams to reinforce memory
- **Teaching**: Sharing builds retention and embodiment

VII. Cognitive and Cultural Considerations

Cognitive Feasibility

- Human experts can recall and perform thousands of patterns over decades (Ericsson et al., 1993)
- Long-term memory improves with emotional connection, repetition, and teaching
- Martial knowledge is embodied, or stored not just mentally but within somatic muscle memory and rhythm

Cultural Challenge

- Modern society favors speed, variety, and instant results
- Systems requiring 20–50 years of investment are often devalued
- Traditional transmission (oral, demonstrated, internalized) is at odds with certification-based or commercialized martial arts

VIII. Can One or a Few Masters Truly Preserve a System This Vast?

✅ Yes - Extraordinary but Not Fantastical

Many **monastic, Daoist,** or **classical lineage** systems have survived due to one or two deeply committed masters per generation. This requires a **lifestyle,** not a hobby. It is not for the casual martial artist—but it is possible and historically supported.

Feasible if the practitioner:

- Lives in immersion
- Teaches regularly
- Revisits the material cyclically
- Structures forms by thematic grouping

However:

- System survival depends on generational transmission
- Modern students may need a modularized curriculum to digest the material
- The original system may evolve, fragment, or reduce as common in many traditions

IX. Hereditary Body Types: Intelligent Design or Marketing Gimmick?

An important aspect of the system under discussion is its claim to include 640 foundational sets distributed across eight hereditary body types. This principle asserts that different forms, drills, or techniques are tailored to suit constitutional differences, physiological predispositions that affect movement mechanics, balance, and energy expression.

8 Different Hereditary Types:

1. Tall
2. Small
3. Overweight
4. Thin
5. Tall and Overweight
6. Small and Overweight
7. Tall and Thin
8. Small and Thin

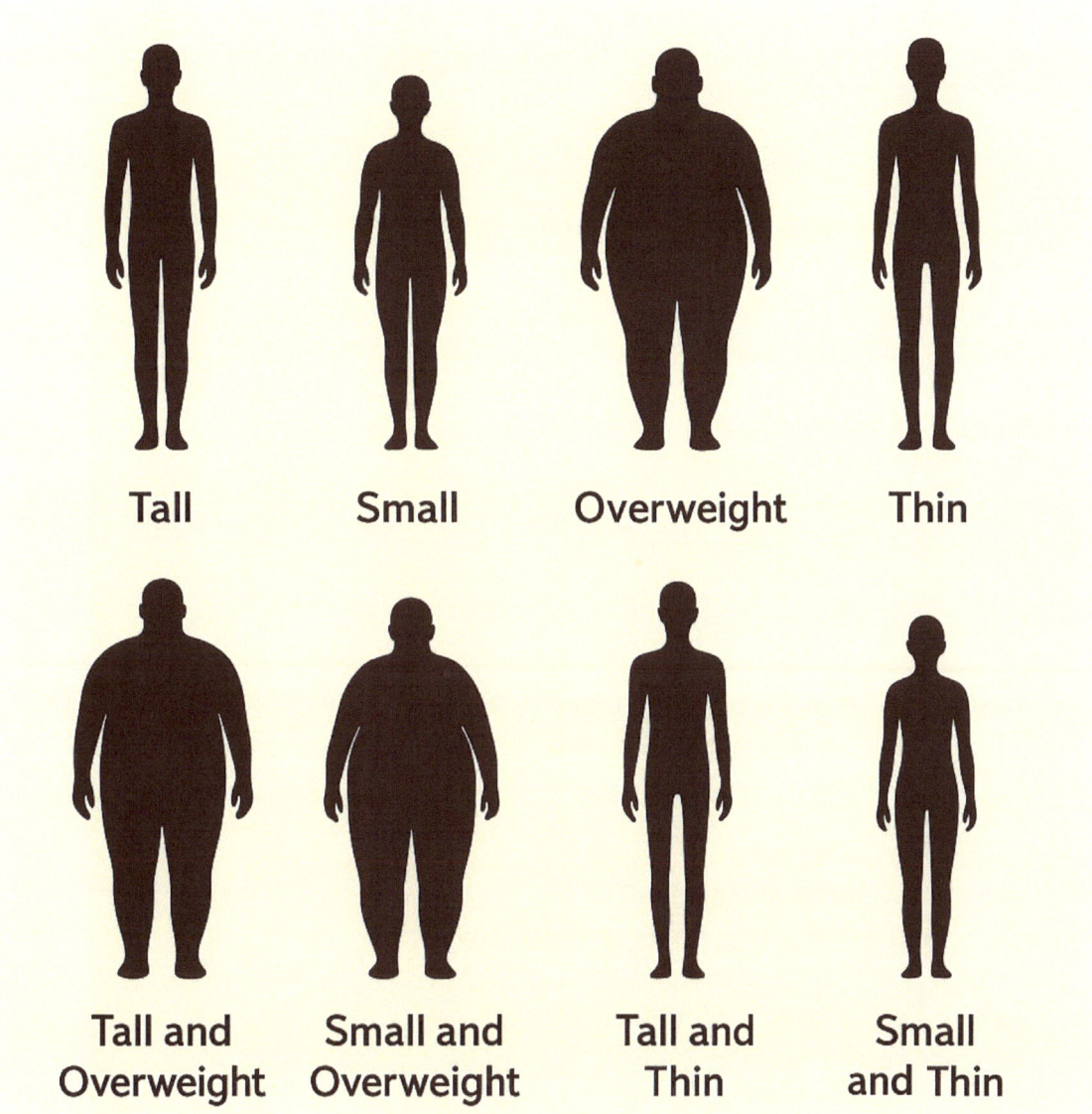

This categorization may seem simplistic at first glance, but it reflects a long-standing tradition in systems such as:

- **Traditional Chinese Medicine (TCM)**: Uses somatotype constitution in diagnosis and qigong prescription.
- **Ayurveda**: Categorizes body-mind types (e.g., Vata, Pitta, Kapha).
- **Martial Lineages**: Where forms were adapted to suit a practitioner's build, power-to-weight ratio, and flexibility.
- **Biomechanical profiling** in sports science

The claim that each of these eight types has access to a specific family of foundational sets suggests a physiologically intelligent system. However, it requires rigorous documentation and consistent application to be credible.

X. Extraordinary Claims Require Extraordinary Evidence

In martial arts and indeed any traditional system, the sheer number of levels, forms, sets, movements, and training layers may raise skepticism, especially when:

- Not recognized by peers
- Lacking written historical lineage
- Missing corroborative physical proof (e.g., preserved manuals, photographic/video documentation, public demonstrations)

Principle of Skepticism:

"Extraordinary claims require extraordinary evidence."
Popularized by Carl Sagan, this principle remains relevant when evaluating martial systems. If a school or master claims:

- 640 unique foundational sets
- 108 specialized Bagua transitions
- Dozens of long forms taking hours to complete

Then, the burden of proof falls upon the claimant to:

- Produce lineage records
- Provide structured curriculum or teaching materials
- Demonstrate practical proficiency in said material

This isn't to challenge the sincerity of the tradition, but rather to reinforce credibility and transparency in a world where esoteric claims are often made without accountability.

XI. The Problem of Deception: Buyer Beware

There are, unfortunately, martial groups and individuals who leverage the allure of ancient, secret, or overly complex systems to:

- Elevate their authority
- Shield scrutiny through obscurity

- Create dependence among students

⚠️ **Red Flags in Questionable Systems:**

- Inability to demonstrate claimed techniques
- Unverifiable lineage (or lineage constantly evolving to fit narrative)
- Overuse of mysticism or secrecy to justify lack of transparency
- Commercial exploitation (e.g., charging for levels with no meaningful advancement)

✅ **Student Guidelines for Due Diligence:**

- Ask for documentation (written, photographic, curriculum outlines)
- Observe public demonstrations or request private proof of capacity
- Cross-reference claims with outside martial scholars or historians
- Follow your intuition. If something feels manipulative, it likely is

True mastery does not hide behind jargon or cult-like authority. It is revealed in clarity, function, humility, and the ability to teach and demonstrate.

XII. Reinforcing a Balanced Perspective

While skepticism is essential, we must not lose sight of this:

Some traditional systems *do* legitimately carry vast knowledge, passed from generation to generation, often in difficult-to-document formats.

However, those systems tend to demonstrate:

- Consistent internal logic
- Observable results
- Coherent pedagogy
- Recognition from external peer groups, even across style lines

In today's environment, a balance between open-mindedness and critical thinking is necessary. One must neither accept everything at face value nor reject ancient systems outright simply because they differ from modern expectations.

XIII. Conclusion

The legacy of vast martial arts systems, those containing hundreds of forms, transitional movements, and specialized adaptations—is not mere fantasy. A system that claims such breadth across hereditary types, multi-hour sequences, and internal development deserves consideration, though never blind belief. When such a tradition stands up to scrutiny, produces capable practitioners, and yields consistent, reproducible results, it holds rightful value as part of our shared martial heritage.

Modern practitioners, teachers, and researchers are encouraged to approach these systems with both open curiosity and informed skepticism. Honoring the tradition while requiring evidence of depth and effectiveness. This is an extraordinary path, one that demands lifelong dedication, internalization, and thoughtful adaptation to modern cultural and physiological realities.

While full memorization or mastery of a massive system may be unrealistic for the average student today, it remains attainable for the truly dedicated individual or lineage holder, especially when approached methodically, over time, and with intelligent curriculum design. In today's time-limited world, success lies not in grasping everything at once, but in embodying enough of the system to preserve and transmit its essential spirit and utility.

If not approached carefully, however, such systems risk becoming exaggerated relics or worse, tools of deception. As always: *Caveat emptor* - buyer beware.

Extraordinary Methods of Kung Practice

(Chow & Spangler, 1982)

References:

Chinese martial arts training manuals : a historical survey : Kennedy, Brian, 1958- : Free Download, Borrow, and Streaming : Internet Archive. (2005). Internet Archive. https://archive.org/details/chinesemartialar0000kenn

Chow, D., & Spangler, R. (1982). *Kung Fu: History, Philosophy, and Technique.*

Chu, F. (2019) *Baguazhang -- Overview.* https://shaolin.org/general-3/research/baguazhang/all.html?utm_source=chatgpt.com

Comprehensive Asian fighting arts : Draeger, Donn F : Free Download, Borrow, and Streaming : Internet Archive. (1980). Internet Archive. https://archive.org/details/comprehensiveasi0000drae

Ericsson, Karl & Krampe, Ralf & Tesch-Roemer, Clemens. (1993). The Role of Deliberate Practice in the Acquisition of Expert Performance. Psychological Review. 100. 363-406. 10.1037//0033-295X.100.3.363.

Henning, S. E. (1999). Academia encounters the Chinese martial arts. *DeepDyve.* https://www.deepdyve.com/lp/university-of-hawai-i-press/academia-encounters-the-chinese-martial-arts-XdDBjABJdT

Sagan, C. (1996). *The Demon-Haunted World: Science as a Candle in the Dark.* New York: Random House.

Shahar, M. (2008). *The Shaolin Monastery: History, Religion, and the Chinese Martial Arts.* University of Hawaii Press.

Shing, T. C. (2020b). *Xiantian Bagua Zhang: Gao Style Bagua Zhang - Circle Form.* Singing Dragon.

Wikipedia contributors. (2025, June 26). *Baguazhang.* Wikipedia. https://en.wikipedia.org/wiki/Baguazhang?utm_source=chatgpt.com

Wikipedia contributors. (2024, July 8). *Neigong.* Wikipedia. https://en.wikipedia.org/wiki/Neigong?utm_source=chatgpt.com

Yang, Jwing-Ming. (1996). *The Root of Chinese Qigong.* YMAA Publications.

Chamsa Meditation

Inner Vision, Pre-Birth Awareness, and the Mirror of Enlightenment

A Korean-Taoist Path of Self-Inquiry and Spiritual Return

Introduction

Within the quiet intersections of Korean martial arts, Seon Buddhism, Taoist inner alchemy, and indigenous contemplative practice, there exists a lesser-known meditative path called **Chamsa (참사)**. Translated loosely as "true reflection" or "sincere contemplation," this practice involves a series of inner visualizations that begin with the face and end with formless awareness. It guides the practitioner from physical identity, through spiritual regression, and into the vast, unconditioned presence that many traditions call enlightenment, *nirvana*, or union with the *Tao*.

Chamsa serves not only as a vehicle of personal transformation but also as a symbolic journey through layers of ego, memory, and form, toward a realization of the true self that was never born and never dies.

I. Origins and Conceptual Foundations

1. Linguistic Meaning

In Korean, **Cham** (참) means "true" or "authentic," while **Sa** (사) may refer to "thought," "contemplation," or "reflection" (Kim, 2018). Thus, Chamsa points to a practice of authentic inward reflection, aligned with the spiritual aim of uncovering the nature of self and reality.

2. Syncretic Influences

The practice bridges three major influences:

- **Seon (Zen) Buddhism**: Emphasizes *hwadu* (Kōan-style inquiry), non-dual awareness, and meditation as a route to awakening (Aitken, 1990; Dumoulin, 2005).
- **Taoist Neidan (inner alchemy)**: Employs visualizations, energy return, and prenatal regression to restore original spirit (Komjathy, 2013; Yang, 1997).
- **Korean shamanic mysticism**: Embraces spiritual vision, ancestral awareness, and altered states as portals to insight (Kim, 2018).

II. The Stages of Chamsa Practice

Chamsa is typically taught as a stage-based meditation, though advanced practitioners may cycle through its phases in a single session. Each stage builds upon the last, guiding the practitioner from concrete visualization to subtle realization.

Stage 1: Face Visualization

- **Description**: Eyes closed, visualize your own face in full, accurate detail, every wrinkle, mole, and asymmetry. Include features such as the slope of the nose, eyebrow placement, asymmetries, scars, skin texture, color, and even the micro-expressions of your resting face. The image should be as vivid and lifelike as if one were looking into a mirror with eyes open.
- **Purpose**: Strengthen *shen* (spirit), develop internal focus, and anchor awareness in the "mind mirror." This aligns with Taoist inner vision practices (nèishì), projecting awareness from the third eye center or upper dantian (Kohn, 1993; Yang, 1997).

Stage 2: Dissolution of the Face

- **Description**: Allow the mental image of the face to gradually blur, dissolve, or melt away without force. Observe any resistance or attachment as the image fades.
- **Purpose**: Cultivate detachment from personal identity and begin breaking down the egoic image of the self. This mirrors both Zen and Taoist instructions for letting go of attachment to form (Dumoulin, 2005).

Stage 3: Witness Inquiry

- **Description**: With the face gone, turn awareness inward and ask: *"Who is seeing this image?"* or *"What remains when the face disappears?"*
- **Purpose**: This self-inquiry parallels Seon (Zen) Buddhism's hwadu method and Taoist "reflection on the void." It shifts attention to the formless witness, revealing the distinction between perception and identification (Aitken,1990).

Stage 4: Womb Regression

- **Description**: Begin to visualize yourself in the womb. Sense the floating, fluid warmth of the pre-birth state. This visualization is not merely symbolic; it is a meditative immersion into pre-verbal, pre-identity awareness.
- **Purpose**: Return to the state of *yuan qi* and *yuan shen* (original energy and spirit), reconnecting with the undisturbed potential of consciousness prior to conditioning. This corresponds to Taoist embryonic breathing, and the process of returning to the origin (Komjathy, 2013).

Stage 5: Original Face

- **Description**: Let go of all visualizations. Abide in spacious presence. Ask: *"What was my original face before my parents were born?"*
- **Purpose**: This stage reflects the heart of Zen realization. All form, memory, and thought dissolve, revealing emptiness and unconditioned awareness (Aitken, 1990).

Stage 6: Return and Integration

- **Description**: Slowly bring awareness back to the breath, body, and senses. Open the eyes and re-engage with the outer world from this clarified state.

- **Purpose**: To integrate realization into daily life. The clarity cultivated through chamsa should inform one's behavior, relationships, and presence, aligning with both Taoist spontaneity and the Zen Ox-herding picture of reentering the world with open hands (Dumoulin, 2005; Yang, 1997).

Chamsa Meditation Progression

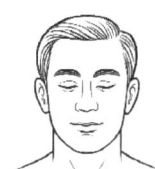  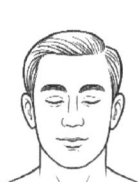 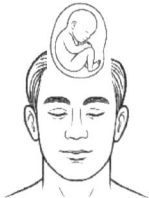 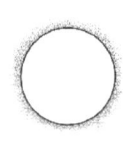 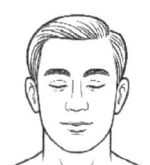

Face Visualization — Eyes closed, visualize your own face in full detail

Dissolution of the Face — Allow the face image to blur, dissolve, fade

Witness Inquiry — Ask, "Who is seeing this image?" or "Who am I?"

Womb Regression — Visualize within your mother's womb

Original Face — Ask, "What was your original face before your parents were born?

Return & Integration — Gently return to your body and the external world

III. Practice Progression: Gradual vs. Cyclical

Progressive Practice (for most practitioners)

Stage	Timeframe	Developmental Aim
Face Visualization	1–2 weeks	Image clarity, stillness
Dissolution	1–2 weeks	Letting go, self-inquiry begins
Inquiry	2+ weeks	Direct experience of the observer
Womb Regression	Variable	Comfort with silence and non-conceptual being
Original Face	Ongoing	Insight into emptiness and non-duality

This mirrors the traditional model used in both Zen training and Taoist alchemical refinement (Komjathy, 2013; Dumoulin, 2005).

Cyclical Practice (for advanced practitioners)

Experienced meditators may move through all stages in a single sitting. This is often employed in advanced *neigong, zazen*, or during spiritual retreats (Yang, 1997).

IV. Chamsa and Enlightenment

1. As a Route to Enlightenment

Chamsa progressively dismantles the layers of self-identity. It leads to *direct realization* of formless presence, making it consistent with both Zen's gradual approach and Taoism's return to source (Aitken,1990; Komjathy, 2013).

2. As an Expression of Enlightenment

At deeper levels, the practice becomes a *reflection of the awakened state*. It is used not to attain enlightenment, but to maintain presence and live from insight (Dumoulin, 2005).

"The enlightened one returns to the marketplace with open hands." — Zen Ox-Herding Picture #10

V. Comparative Models of Enlightenment

Aspect	Chamsa	Zen Buddhism	Taoist Alchemy	Tibetan Dzogchen
Starting Point	Visualization of face	Hwadu or breath focus	Jing → Qi → Shen transmutation	Rigpa recognition
Key Turning Point	Dissolution and womb regression	"Great doubt" or koan resolution	Return to origin	Breakthrough to spontaneous presence
Final Aim	Witnessing the "original face"	Satori, then integration	Unity with Tao	Recognition of non-dual awareness
Method	Visual inquiry & regression	Self-inquiry & zazen	Breath, energy, visualization	Direct pointing-out instruction
Expression	Calm presence, embodied wisdom	Actionless action, compassion	Spontaneity, longevity, clarity	Effortless awareness, freedom

VI. Conclusion: Returning to the Formless Mirror

Chamsa meditation is both a method and a metaphor: a way of seeing the self by watching it dissolve. It begins with the familiar image of the face and guides the practitioner back to the unconditioned awareness before identity, thought, and time.

Whether used as a route to insight or a means of stabilization, Chamsa bridges Korean, Taoist, and Buddhist traditions. It reveals that the journey inward is not a retreat, but a return to that which has always been present.

"To know the self is to forget the self. To forget the self is to be enlightened by all things."
— Dōgen Zenji, *Genjōkōan*

References:

Aitken, R. (1990). *The Gateless Barrier: The Wu-Men Kuan (Mumonkan)*. North Point Press.
https://archive.org/details/gatelessbarrierw0000aitk

Dumoulin, H. (2005). *Zen Buddhism: A History (Vol. 2: Japan)*. World Wisdom. Zen Buddhism : a history : Dumoulin, Heinrich : Free Download, Borrow, and Streaming : Internet Archive

Kim, C. (2018). Korean shamanism. In *Routledge eBooks*.
https://doi.org/10.4324/9781315198156

Kohn, L. (1993). *The Taoist Experience: An Anthology*. SUNY Press.
https://archive.org/details/thetaoistexperienceliviakohn

Komjathy, L. (2013). *The Daoist Tradition: An Introduction*. Bloomsbury Academic.
https://www.bloomsbury.com/us/daoist-tradition-9781441168733/

Yang, J. (1997). *The Root of Chinese Qigong: Secrets of Health, Longevity, and Enlightenment*. YMAA.
https://archive.org/details/therootofchineseqigongbyyangjwingming1997

Degrees of Control: Psychological Lessons from a Closed Community

The Boiling Frog of Belonging: How High-Control Groups Capture Us

A Journey Through Martial Arts, Immersion, and Awakening

Many people enter martial arts schools, spiritual communities, or exclusive organizations seeking fitness, discipline, purpose, or belonging. Yet what begins with training can, in some cases, evolve into an insular, high control, closed environment that slowly demands total conformity. This article integrates firsthand experiences with sociocultural analysis, exploring how these dynamics unfold, how they draw in even intelligent and educated individuals, and how they can be recognized and overcome.

Because humans often have short memories of uncomfortable truths we'd rather not acknowledge. When we fail to remember or record history, we invite it to repeat. Revisiting these experiences today helps us confront patterns that could otherwise recur unchallenged. While most people grow older, they do not necessarily grow wiser. Physical age and mental growth or wisdom do not always increase together. I want to believe that people and their behaviors can change and evolve for the better. A caterpillar eventually transforms into a butterfly. Yet we must also recognize that, as the saying goes, "*a tiger cannot change its stripes*."

I am not sharing this to assign blame, demand accountability, or even to provide perfect clarity. Everyone who was involved knows, to some degree, what transpired. I do not see myself as a victim; I, too, was a willing participant for two decades, rationalizing along the way that the *"ends would justify the means,"* until I chose to stop being compliant. Today, it matters less to me whether others have changed or evolved, as that is their path, their journey, and their challenge to resolve within themselves. What matters most is what I have learned and earned. Inner transformation and self-mastery, ironically, can emerge in spite of, or perhaps because of, the very circumstances we experience firsthand.

What makes me qualified to speak on this topic?
I was deeply involved in a high-control closed martial arts group for 20 years, serving in positions of authority as a senior-level instructor, mid-to-upper management, and as an owner of multiple locations. Years later, after decades of research, conducting numerous interviews with individuals from diverse backgrounds both within and beyond the martial arts world, and pursuing higher education, I believe I am a credible resource to speak on this topic.

Part I: How High-Control Martial Arts & Other Groups Draw You In

The Bait: Personal Desires and the Illusion of Fulfillment
High-control closed groups thrive by mirroring what potential members most deeply want: strength, mastery, inner peace, community, etc. They craft an environment that reflects those desires, creating a powerful sense of destiny and belonging. As described in one firsthand account:

"I was a discontent 19-year-old, searching for meaning in a world that felt broken. The school I found promised not just martial arts but enlightenment, peace, and brotherhood. They offered exactly what I was longing for, and I was hooked."

Different Experiences, Different Interpretations
It's essential to recognize that not everyone in a high-control environment shares the same experience, even when standing in the same room. Individual memories and interpretations are shaped by personal histories, perceptions, and expectations, like siblings recalling the same childhood differently as adults. Many members gained meaningful benefits from training in this system, including friendships, exposure to Asian culture, and valuable traits such as cultivating a "can-do attitude." Others, however, experienced harm and disillusionment. Ironically, one of my own most significant lessons was learning how **not** to treat or interact with other people, especially recognizing the importance of never taking advantage of others for personal gain. Both positive and negative perspectives are real, valid, and necessary to understand the full picture.

The Con: How Desire Enables Entrapment
The foundation of any effective con is mutual participation: it cannot succeed unless the "mark" wants what's being offered. In high-control martial arts environments, the leadership uses students' own goals to pull them deeper. It's not that people don't see the red flags; it's that they rationalize them away because the group appears to offer what they crave most. This is why even highly educated professionals, trained to think critically, can fall prey. They are often convinced they're fulfilling a noble or enlightened purpose.

High Achievers Are Not Immune
Doctors, lawyers, college professors, firefighters, law enforcement, and other accomplished and educated professionals are just as susceptible to immersion in high-control environments as anyone else. This group strived to bring these types of people into the fold, not only for their income but also their access to power, influence, and other resources. It is a mistake to assume that education or social status alone shields a person from manipulation. In fact, those with strong ambitions, high standards, or deep desires for excellence can be especially vulnerable when a group appears to promise fulfillment of those ideals.

Overconfidence and the Dunning-Kruger Effect
Another factor that can blind even intelligent, capable individuals to a high-control group's manipulation is the Dunning-Kruger Effect, a cognitive bias in which people with limited knowledge or experience overestimate their competence (Dunning & Kruger, 1999). This misplaced confidence can lead new members, or even seasoned instructors who've gained some amount of knowledge, to believe they fully understand martial arts, philosophy, or personal development more deeply than they actually do, leaving them vulnerable to manipulation.

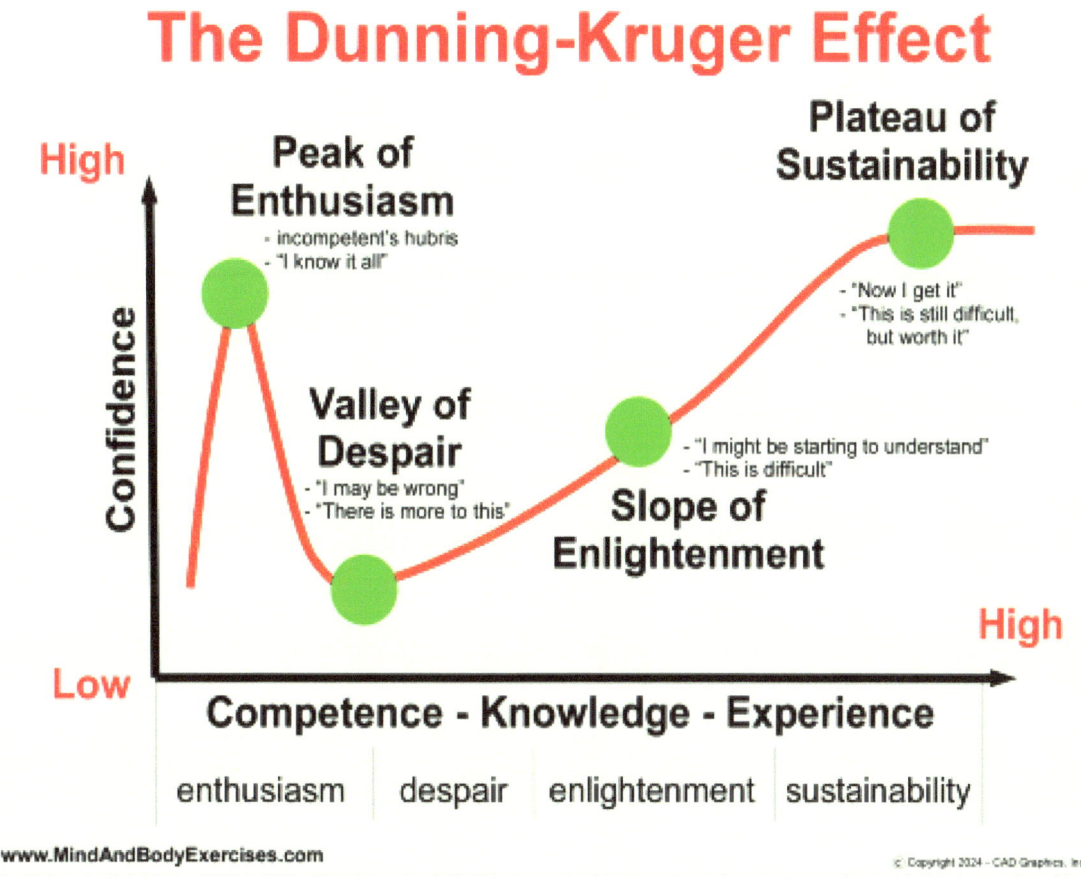

The Immersion by Degrees: Small Steps Toward Total Commitment
High-control groups rarely show their true face at first. They escalate demands gradually. Small favors become hours of service; a few classes become total life dedication. This mirrors the *boiling frog metaphor*: a frog placed in cool water that is slowly heated will fail to notice the danger until it is too late (Hoffer, 1951). In high-control groups, each incremental step normalizes the next, shifting members' sense of what is acceptable and desirable. One signs up to become stronger, better, more confident. But in time, they find themselves painting houses, fixing cars, cutting lawns, and picking apples from trees. Others, even those considered high-level 7th- and 8th-degree martial arts practitioners, found themselves at the

grandmaster's beck and call, running errands, picking up his children from school, or maintaining homes late into the night for other members of the grandmaster's family. And even others would come to find out that their wives were being violated by the grandmaster (as alleged by multiple high-level former members) while they were away handling other school business. But they all originally signed up because they just wanted to be *better*.

The Demand: Conformity and Life Domination
A high-control environment crosses a critical line when it demands:
- Adoption of the group's beliefs as absolute truth.
- Isolation from family, friends, and outside perspectives.
- Complete control over finances, living arrangements, and time.

As one former member described:

"My days extended to 16, even 22 hours of training, chores, and teaching. I stopped seeing friends. My world shrank to the group and its leadership. Doubt became synonymous with betrayal"

Part II: The Mechanics of Control – Testing, Indoctrination, and Financial Exploitation

The Tests: Can You Be Controlled?
Early tests appear benign: running errands, buying lunch/dinner, staying late, or accepting unusual requests. Compliance opens the door to greater demands such as:

- *"Do you know someone?"*
- *"Can you access some information?"*
- *"How hard would it be to….?*

Each act reinforces members' willingness to surrender autonomy.

Indoctrination Through Exhaustion
After grueling physical sessions, mental and emotional defenses are lowered. Doctrinal messages "Only we know the truth," "Others won't understand," are then delivered. This alternating pattern of exhaustion and indoctrination is a hallmark of high-control environments (Lifton, 1961). Intense physical exhaustion impairs critical thinking by depleting cognitive resources (Hockey, 2013), while acetylcholine enhances selective attention to salient stimuli, such as a leader's directives (Sarter et al., 2006). Under fatigue, chaotic neural dynamics further disrupt prefrontal cortex function (Freeman, 1994), reducing skepticism and increasing reliance on group authority. This neurobiological triad (exhaustion + hyperfocus + disrupted judgment) creates fertile ground for compliance.

Financial Exploitation

High-control martial arts and self-help groups often sell an endless series of advanced courses, each promising unique secrets and requiring ever-larger payments. Promotions and rank tests become both a symbol of loyalty and a financial trap. Students believe they are climbing a ladder to mastery when in reality they are climbing deeper into dependence.

Part III: Recognizing the Trap – Signs of an Insular, High-Control Dynamic

Shifts from Enthusiasm to Dependency
- When training becomes the center of identity, eclipsing other relationships and interests.
- When intuitive feelings of unease are rationalized away: *"I've come too far to turn back now."*

Isolation from Outside Perspectives
- Members are discouraged or forbidden from studying with other teachers or seeking alternative viewpoints.
- Outsiders are framed as confused, ignorant, misguided, or even enemies.
- This dynamic reflects classic groupthink theory, where pressure for conformity and insulation from dissenting voices fosters poor decision-making and blind loyalty (Janis, 1972).

Hierarchy and Absolute Authority
- A central leader portrayed as infallible.
- This reflects what sociologist Max Weber described as "charismatic authority," where devotion to an individual perceived as extraordinary cements hierarchical control (Weber, 1947).
- Senior members policing behavior and loyalty.

Total Lifestyle Control
- Living with fellow members to ensure surveillance and group reinforcement.
- Careers guided or manipulated to keep members financially tied to the group.

When the Most Loyal Turned Away

Fourteen upper-management instructors, including the grandmaster at the top of this organization, were incarcerated for federal crimes. Most served approximately 4.5 years in federal prison. Upon their release, only four members returned to the grandmaster's tutelage. The other eight former managers broke with the organization entirely, with some going on to mentor others about the abuses they once participated in or witnessed. Some of those have seemingly fallen off the face of the earth and want no contact with anyone ever connected to this group.

This is significant because these individuals were among the most loyal to the founder and considered the most qualified high-level practitioners. Many who once enforced the system's harshest controls were later speaking out against it or at least demonstrating their rejection by refusing to return to the *"old school ways."*

I personally knew and learned from most of the top instructors who were later incarcerated. For some, I trained with them only occasionally, but with others, I studied under them extensively for many years. I benefited greatly from these individuals, as I genuinely liked them and deeply respected their martial arts abilities and knowledge. However, as I grew wiser and recognized that many of them lacked a moral compass or treated serious ethical matters flippantly, it became increasingly difficult to accept their guidance on life, direction, or any discussions of morality and ethics.

Over time, I came to respect those who left the group at this level, realizing they had developed the ability to distinguish between what was true, right, and correct.

Addressing *"That Was Then, This Is Now"*

Some current leaders of this organization may claim, *"That was then; this is now,"* suggesting that the abuses of the past are no longer relevant because the individuals responsible are gone. Yet a closer look reveals a different reality: today's upper management includes original managers who were themselves incarcerated for their roles in the organization's wrongdoing, or others who, while not imprisoned, were fully aware of or complicit in the questionable practices that occurred.

There was an overwhelming degree of coercion, deception, and manipulation originating from the top members of this organization. Whether the grandmaster directly orchestrated this behavior, actively encouraged it, was complicit by turning a blind eye, or though least likely, was entirely oblivious to these actions, the result is deeply troubling. Regardless of the explanation, such widespread misconduct stands in stark contrast to the image of someone claiming to embody high moral character or serve as a spiritual leader.

This continuity of leadership raises important questions about whether the group has truly changed, or whether the same patterns of control, secrecy, and abuse remain embedded in its structure. If behaviors have truly changed, how sad that self-reflection only came about due to so many sincere, good-hearted and well-meaning people having left this organization.

Part IV: The Battle Between Intuition and Rationalization

A key insight from my experiences is the conflict between gut instinct and self-justification. Early in immersion, most members sense subtle discomfort. Something feels "off." But instead of heeding this intuition, they explain it away:

- *"This level of discipline is just what I need."*
- *"Everyone else seems fine; I must be the one with doubts."*

This process of cognitive dissonance causes people to ignore warning signs and deepen their commitment (Festinger et al., 1956). The greater the investment, the harder it becomes to acknowledge the truth.

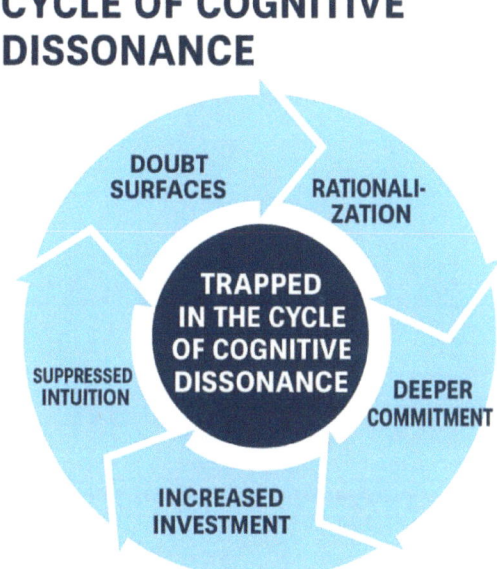

Part V: The Boiling Frog – Immersion by Degrees

The vivid use of the boiling frog metaphor deserves emphasis:

> *"Each step was only slightly more extreme than the last. By the time we faced bizarre or abusive practices, they felt normal compared to yesterday"*

This gradualism makes high-control groups especially dangerous: they do not demand total loyalty overnight, but cultivate it through subtle, cumulative steps. This pattern of gradual escalation aligns with the "foot-in-the-door" technique described in social psychology, where compliance with small requests increases the likelihood of agreeing to larger ones over time (Freedman & Fraser, 1966).

It's important to recognize the significant difference between incremental indoctrination or grooming, where gradual exposure is used to normalize harmful or abusive dynamics and incremental training of the mind, body, and spirit, which is a deliberate progression designed to foster genuine improvement and self-mastery. True martial arts and self-mastery types of instruction should guide students through gradual challenges to build skills, confidence, and character, not to manipulate or erode their autonomy.

Part VI: Parallels Across Culture – Sports, Religion, and Beyond

"One person's culture is another person's cult."

This saying captures how rituals, loyalty, and hierarchical structures can feel like supportive traditions to some, yet oppressive or manipulative to others. Recognizing these parallels helps us understand that intense commitment or exclusive practices are not inherently abusive, but can become dangerous when questioning is discouraged, outsiders are demonized, and absolute loyalty is demanded.

Reflections on sports and religion show similarly how rituals, specialized jargon, uniforms, and passionate loyalty exist in many groups that are not inherently harmful. Sports fans, military units, and religious communities often foster unity through shared traditions. Yet, as we can observe, these elements can be twisted when groups:

- Discourage outside perspectives.
- Frame dissenters as unworthy.
- Require absolute loyalty.

This parallels research showing that when group dynamics become rigid, they can turn into echo chambers where questioning is stifled (Kottak, 2019; Peretz & Fox, 2021).

Part VII: Breaking Free – The Psychological Struggle

Seeing the Truth
Admitting a group's true nature can be harder than enduring it. Even overwhelming external evidence (e.g., investigative exposés) may initially be rejected. As one former member recounted:

> *"I saw a week-long investigative series revealing our group's abuses. My first reaction was outrage — at the reporters. It took time for reality to break through the indoctrination"*

Reassessing the Dream
Leaving often requires reassessing the fantasy that drew one in. This is difficult, as these dreams shape identity. Letting go feels like losing oneself, but it is a necessary step toward recovery.

Rebuilding Identity
Breaking free means redefining oneself outside the group's narratives:

- Recognizing what skills and lessons can be retained without toxic elements.
- Building new relationships.
- Pursuing goals based on personal values, not imposed ideology.

Part VIII: Lessons Learned – Value and Resilience

Experiences in high-control groups can leave scars but also forge strength. Discipline, perseverance, and mental resilience gained through hardship can serve individuals well after they leave. As one survivor noted:

"What most see as problems today are nothing compared to what I survived. It taught me I could face anything"

Post-Traumatic Growth: Transforming Adversity into Strength

While surviving a high-control environment can leave lasting scars, it can also create an opportunity for post-traumatic growth (PTG). PTG refers to positive psychological change experienced as a result of struggling with challenging circumstances (Tedeschi & Calhoun, 2004). For some, leaving an abusive or manipulative group can spur a newfound personal strength, deeper relationships, openness to new possibilities, and a greater appreciation for life. Recognizing these possibilities can empower survivors to move beyond their past, knowing their experiences do not define who they are, but can shape them into wiser, more resilient individuals.

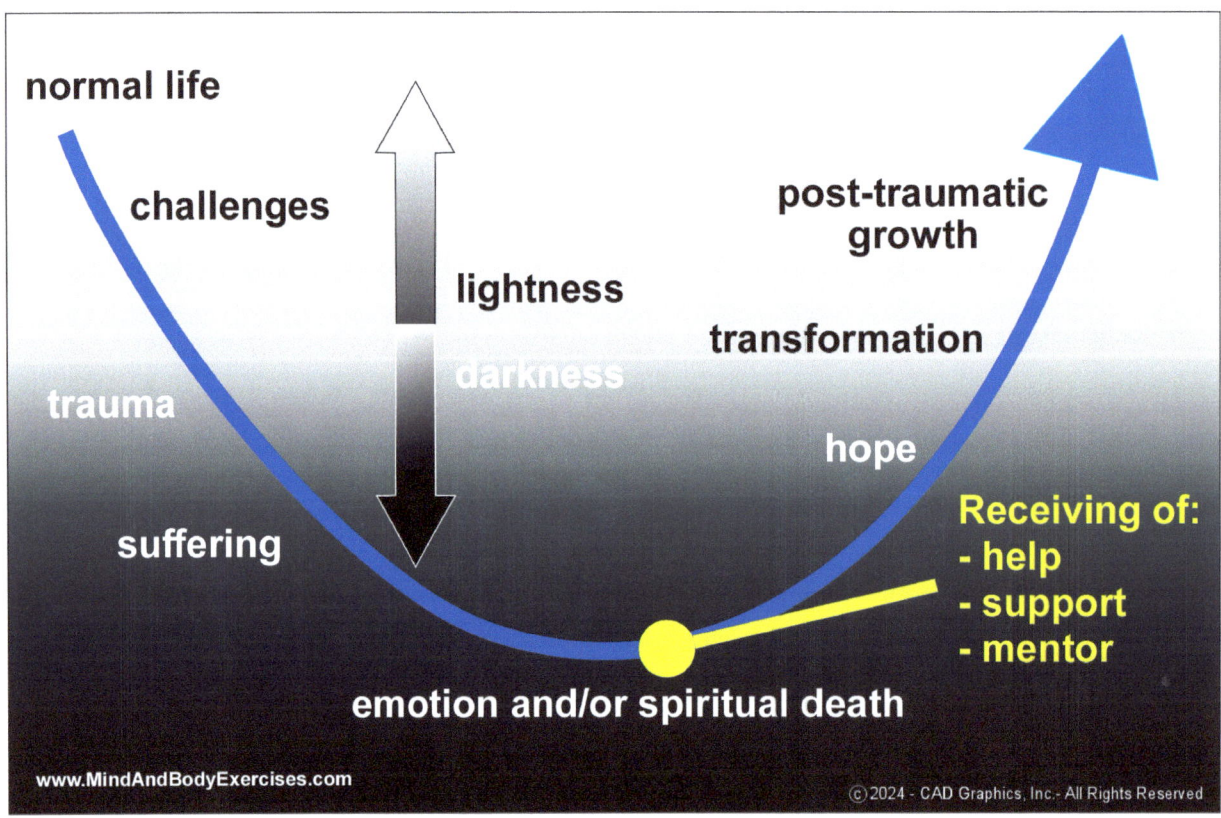

Part IX: Beyond Martial Arts – Creating Ethical Communities

Not every passionate or exclusive group is dangerous. Closed groups can preserve traditions and foster focused learning, but also exist within ethical communities:

- ✅ Encourage critical thinking and questions.
- ✅ Allow members to seek outside perspectives.
- ✅ Balance loyalty with autonomy.
- ✅ Maintain transparency about teachings and leadership.

Healthy Group

Healthy Group	High-Control Group
• Encourages questions	• Discourages questions
• Promotes external perspectives	• Demonizes outside knowledge
• Flexible membership	• Demands total loyalty
• Clear ethical boundaries	• Blurs lines between right and wrong

Conclusion

Those that need to hear of this information will have read this far. Those unwilling to consider these facts may remain in denial, but this work is here for those ready to see. High-control dynamics can emerge in any setting, from martial arts schools to religious organizations or corporate cultures. Recognizing signs of manipulation, immersion by degrees, discouraging outside viewpoints, financial exploitation, etc. Authentic communities foster growth through openness, humility, and respect, not fear or blind loyalty. They seek to empower individuals to protect themselves and others.

References:

Dunning, D., & Kruger, J. (1999). Unskilled and unaware of it: How difficulties in recognizing one's own incompetence lead to inflated self-assessments. *Journal of Personality and Social Psychology, 77*(6), 1121–1134. https://doi.org/10.1037/0022-3514.77.6.1121

Festinger, L., Riecken, H. W., & Schachter, S. (1956). *When Prophecy Fails.* Harper-Torchbooks.

Freeman W. J. (1994). Role of chaotic dynamics in neural plasticity. *Progress in brain research*, *102*, 319–333. https://doi.org/10.1016/S0079-6123(08)60549-X

Freedman, J. L., & Fraser, S. C. (1966). Compliance without pressure: The foot-in-the-door technique. *Journal of Personality and Social Psychology, 4*(2), 195–202. https://doi.org/10.1037/h0023552

Hockey, R. (2013). *The psychology of fatigue.* Cambridge University Press. DOI: 10.1017/CBO9781139015394

Hoffer, E. (1951). *The True Believer: Thoughts on the Nature of Mass Movements.* Harper.

Janis, I. L. (1972). *Victims of groupthink: A psychological study of foreign-policy decisions and fiascoes.* Houghton Mifflin.

Kottak, C. P. (2019). *Mirror for Humanity: A Concise Introduction to Cultural Anthropology.* McGraw-Hill.

Peretz, E., & Fox, J. A. (2021). Religious discrimination against groups perceived as cults in Europe and the West. *Politics, Religion & Ideology, 22*(3-4), 415–435. https://doi.org/10.1080/21567689.2021.1969921

Sarter, M., Gehring, W. J., & Kozak, R. (2006). More attention must be paid: the neurobiology of attentional effort. *Brain research reviews*, *51*(2), 145–160. https://doi.org/10.1016/j.brainresrev.2005.11.002

Statista. (2023, May 4). Sports fans share in the U.S. 2023. https://www.statista.com/statistics/300148/interest-nfl-football-age-canada/

Tedeschi, R. G., & Calhoun, L. G. (2004). Posttraumatic growth: Conceptual foundations and empirical evidence. *Psychological Inquiry, 15*(1), 1–18. https://doi.org/10.1207/s15327965pli1501_01

YPulse. (2023, June 15). NA vs WE: Who Are the Bigger Sports Fans? https://www.ypulse.com/article/2022/05/19/we-na-vs-we-who-are-the-bigger-sports-fans/

SECTION IV: APPENDICES
Sources & Influences

The teachings in this book were not discovered in a single moment of insight. They were lived, tested, remembered, and refined over decades, through movement and meditation, instruction and introspection, guidance from wise mentors and direct confrontation with failure and challenge.

Though these teachings are personal, they do not arise in isolation. They are shaped by an integrated body of philosophical, spiritual, and practical traditions. Below are the major lineages that have informed this body of work:

Confucian Ethics

- The deep emphasis on self-cultivation, duty to family, respectful relationships, and honoring one's teacher are foundational to Confucianism.

- Its relevance is seen in the insistence on integrity, right action, and building a life that honors lineage, legacy, and communal good.

- The mentor as a moral parent and ethical guide echoes the *Analects*, in which the development of virtue is seen as life's highest calling.

Taoist (Daoist) Wisdom

- Taoism's reverence for the natural world, spontaneity, flow, and non-resistance forms the spine of this manuscript's internal cultivation philosophy.

- Practices such as Tai Chi, Qigong and BaguaZhang come directly from Taoist ideas about harmony with the cosmos, internal alchemy, and the movement of qi.

- The symbolic use of wind, fire, and water in the cultivation of personal transformation and the emphasis on *wu wei* (non-forcing) are central Taoist motifs.

Buddhist & Zen Insight

- Meditation, impermanence, ego-transcendence, and the path of non-attachment are Buddhist contributions found throughout.

- The teachings on suffering as a teacher, and silence as a revealer of truth, are drawn from Zen (Chan) practice.

- The concept of the "empty vessel" and the "seed of peace" are meditative metaphors rooted in monastic wisdom traditions.

Martial Arts Philosophy & Warrior Codes

- The practical framework for discipline, hierarchy, and personal mastery emerges from East Asian martial codes including *Bushidō* and *Hwa Rang Do*.

- Martial systems such as BaguaZhang, Qigong, Tai Chi, and Korean Neigong shape the internal foundation of this work, in training energy, breath, posture, and presence.

- The triangle of student-teacher-God echoes long-standing warrior traditions emphasizing humility, loyalty, and service beyond the self.

Spiritual Psychology & Mind-Body Integration

- Concepts such as inner guarding, cognitive discipline, and mental reframing reflect modern psychological perspectives (particularly Jungian and transpersonal).

- Somatic practices, breath regulation, and mindfulness techniques are integrated from holistic health systems that unite body, mind, and spirit.

- The idea that "you shape reality through awareness and discipline" mirrors both mystical psychology and modern neuroplasticity research.

- Reflections on emotional wounds, post-traumatic growth, resilience, and healing align with modern somatic psychology, polyvagal theory, and transpersonal development models.

- Concepts like wounded healers, misogi, and internalized shame are discussed using a language that bridges ancient wisdom with current therapeutic models.

Philosophy of Truth, Morality, and Awareness

- The essays on True, Right, and Correct, perception, and moral discernment integrate principles from ethics, logic, epistemology, and applied philosophy.
- The balance of thought, feeling, and spiritual intuition shows clear parallels to Jungian psychology, Stoicism, and Eastern logic systems.

Theological Themes & Christian Reflection

- Moral clarity, divine accountability, spiritual judgment, and sowing-and-reaping principles reflect shared themes in Christianity, Judaism, Islam, and Sufism.

- The framing of life as a test, the unseen as eternal, and service as the highest act all align with Abrahamic spiritual ethics.

- Commentary on organized religion, the role of Jesus as a spiritual rebel, and the metaphors of heaven reflect a post-institutional yet reverent theological view.

- Biblical motifs such as sowing and reaping, the Upside-Down King, and "bringing heaven with us" express a personal, principle-based spirituality.

Cultural and Linguistic Perspectives

- Exploration of Korean terms like *jeong, uri,* and *chamsa,* and essays on camaraderie and social cohesion reflect your lived cross-cultural knowledge.
- The philosophical unpacking of modern vs. traditional rites of passage, martial brotherhood, and intergenerational wisdom show your understanding of ethnosociological dynamics

Final Note

Though this book is influenced by multiple traditions, it is bound to none. Its purpose is not to convert or convince, but rather to awaken, to strengthen, and to guide.

If you resonate with these teachings, it is likely because the truth they point to already lives within you. This manuscript simply offers a mirror and a map.

Walk forward with clarity. Return to your root. And may the peace you cultivate within ripple outward into a world ready to receive it.

Glossary

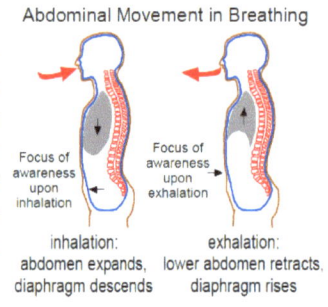

Abdominal Movement in Breathing
Focus of awareness upon inhalation
Focus of awareness upon exhalation
inhalation: abdomen expands, diaphragm descends
exhalation: lower abdomen retracts, diaphragm rises

Abdominal breathing – effective, diaphragmatic breathing that fills your lungs fully, reaches all the way down to your abdomen, slows your breathing rate, and helps you relax.

Bagua (or Pa Kua) / 8-trigrams - eight symbols used in Daoist philosophy to represent the fundamental principles of reality, seen as a range of eight interrelated concepts. Each consists of three lines, each line either "broken" or "unbroken," respectively representing yin or yang.

Ch'ien Heaven
Tui Valley / Lake
Sun Wind
Li Fire
K'an Water
Chen Thunder
Ken Mountain
K'un Earth

The Brass Basin – sits within the lower abdomen, touching at the navel in the front, between L2 & L3 vertebrae in the back and the perineum at the base.

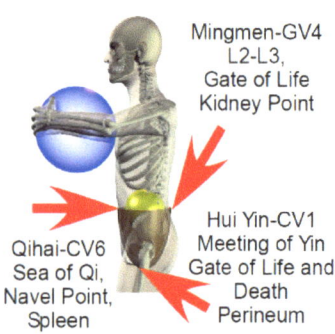

Mingmen-GV4 L2-L3, Gate of Life Kidney Point
Qihai-CV6 Sea of Qi, Navel Point, Spleen
Hui Yin-CV1 Meeting of Yin Gate of Life and Death Perineum

Bubbling Well - an energetic point located in the sole of the foot, slightly in front of the arch between the 2nd and 3rd toe. In the meridian system it is the same as the Kidney 1 point.

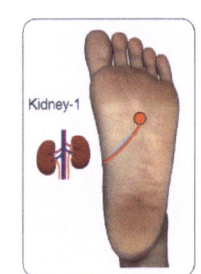

Kidney-1

Dan Tian - 3 energy centers Lower Dan Tian (1 of 3) - also known as the "sea of qi," is positioned below and behind the naval encompassing your lower bowl and is closely related to jing (or physical essence).

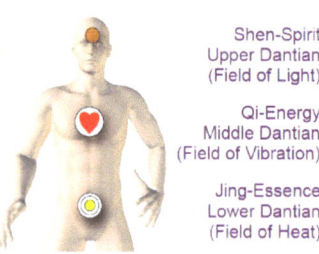

Shen-Spirit Upper Dantian (Field of Light)
Qi-Energy Middle Dantian (Field of Vibration)
Jing-Essence Lower Dantian (Field of Heat)

Daoyin, DaoYi, Daoist Yoga, Qigong – all names for energy exercises, with specific postures, little or no physical body movement and mindful regulated breathing patterns.

Feng Shui – translated into 'wind and water'; it is a Chinese philosophical system that teaches how to balance the energies in any given space.

FENG wind
SHUI water

Conception Vessel (Ren Mai) – flows up the midline of the front of the body and governs all of the yin channels. The Conception Vessel is connected to the Thrusting and Yin Linking vessels.

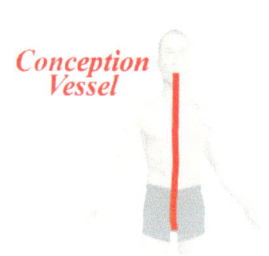

Conception Vessel

Governing Vessel (Du Mai) - flows up the midline of the back and governs all the Yang channels.

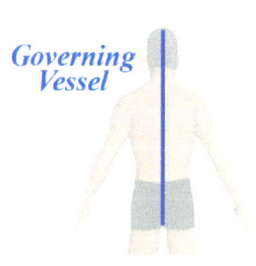

Governing Vessel

General Yu Fei – creator of the 8 Pieces of Brocade set.

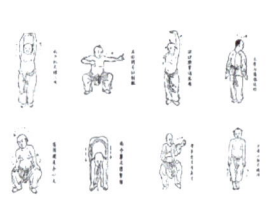

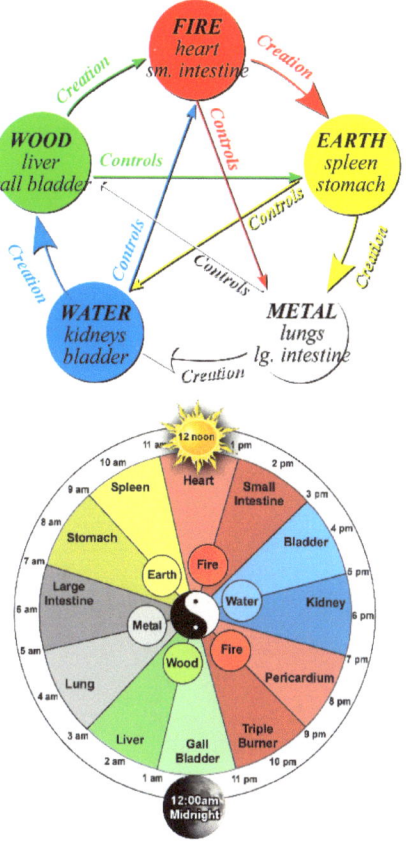

Controlling Cycle – the controlling or regulating sequence of the 5 element cycle. Wood controls Earth; Earth controls Water; Water controls Fire; Fire controls Metal; Metal controls Wood

Generating Cycle – the creative sequence of the 5 element cycle. Wood generates Fire; Fire generates Earth; Earth generates Metal; Metal generates Water; Water generates Wood.

Horary Cycle - 24 Hour Qi Flow Though the Meridians; This cycle is known as the Horary cycle or the Circadian Clock. As Qi (energy) makes its way through the meridians, each meridian in turn with its associated organ, has a two-hour period during which it is at maximum energy.

Jing Well - The Jing (Well) points are 1 of 5 of The Five Element Points (shu) of the 12 energy meridians. They are located on the fingers and toes of the four extremities. These points are thought to be where the Qi of the meridians emerges and begins moving towards the trunk of the body. These are of upmost importance in that these points can help restore balance within the energy flow throughout the human body.

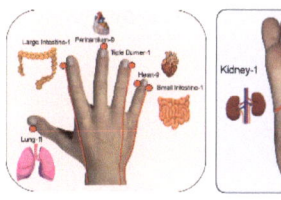 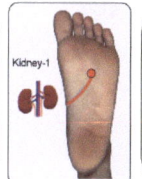 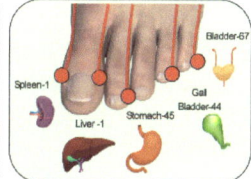

Meridians - a meridian is an 'energy highway' in the human body. There are 12 meridians and each is paired with an organ. Qi energy flows through these meridians or energy highways.

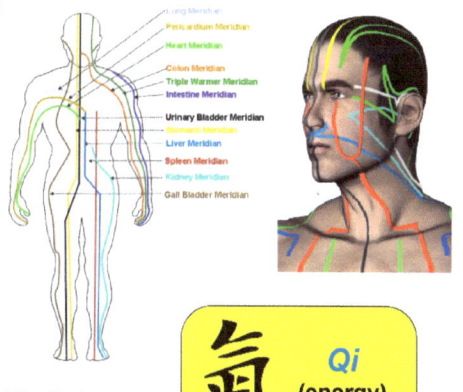

Qigong - or Chi Kung, is breathing exercises, with little or no body movement, that can adjust the brain waves to the Alpha state. When the mind is relaxed, the body chemistry changes and promotes natural healing.

San Jiao (Triple Burner/Heater) – is a meridian line that regulates respiration, digestion and elimination. It is responsible for the movement and transformation of various solids and fluids throughout the system, as well as for the production and circulation of nourishing and protective energy.

Upper Burner	WEI QI
Middle Burner	YING QI
Lower Burner	YUAN QI

Nine Gates - the energy gates in your body are major relay stations where the strength of your Qi are regulated. These gates are located at joints or, more precisely, in the actual space between the bones of a joint. The nine gates are located at the shoulder, elbow and wrists, hip, knee and ankles, and along the cervical, the thoracic, and the lumbar spine.

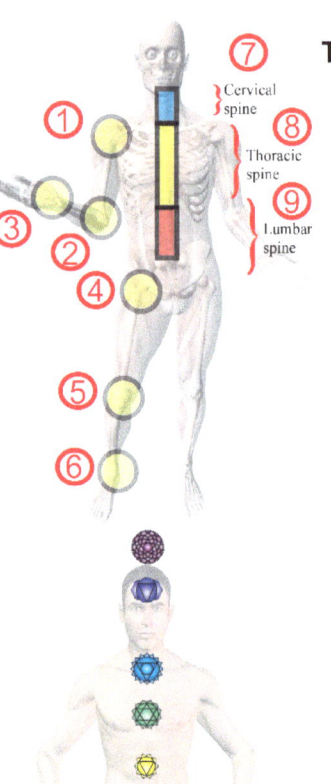

Three Treasures – Jing, Qi & Shen

Jing – (essence) the physical, yin and most dense of the Three Treasures. Think of Jing as a candle, specifically the quality and quantity of the wax.

Qi, chi or ki - (energy/breath) the energetic, vital force within all living things and it the most refined Treasure. Think of Qi as the burning flame of the candle.

Shen – (consciousness or spirit, is the most subtle of the Three Treasures and is the vitality behind Jing and Qi. Think of Shen as the light or illumination produced from the flame.

Seven Energy Centers – also known as chakras, are energy points in the subtle body that start at the base of the spinal column, continue through the sacral, solar plexus, heart, throat, eyebrow and end in the midst of the head vertex at the crown.

Six Healing Sounds – auditory sounds used for clearing internal (yin) organs and other tissues of stagnant Qi.

Metal - Hissss	Water - Chuuu	Wood - Shiiiii	Fire - Haaaa	Earth - Hoooo	6th Qi - Heeee
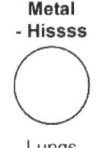					
Lungs Lg. Intestine	Kidneys Bladder	Liver Gall Bladder	Heart Sm. Intestine	Spleen Stomach	Pericardium Triple Burner

The 3 Hearts – Heart, abdomen, calves: The first heart is the heart in your chest for the oxygenation of the blood. Lower abdominal breathing is considered the second heart for circulation of fluid, Qi and digestion. The third heart is the calf muscles for re-circulation of the blood.

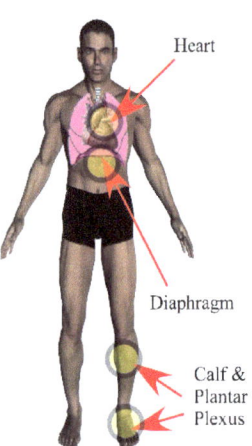

Small Circuit – the linking two energy pathways that run along the midline of the body into a cycling loop. The "fire pathway", Du Mai (Governing Vessel), extends up the back and the other, Ren Mai (Conception Vessel), down the front of the body.

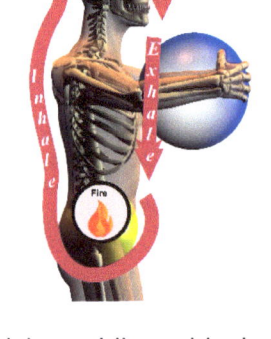

Vessels – there are 8 extraordinary vessels that function as reservoirs of Qi for the Twelve Regular Meridians.

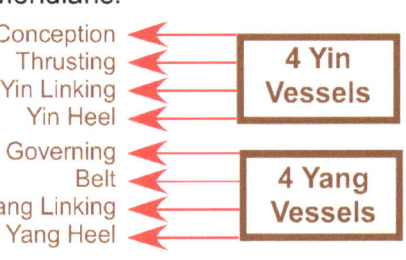

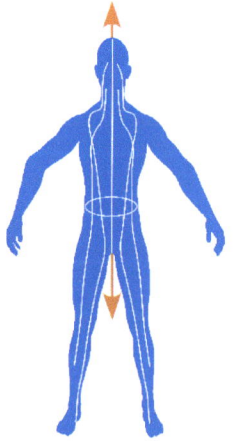

Taoism - (sometimes Daoism) is a philosophical or ethical tradition of Chinese origin, or faith of Chinese exemplification, that emphasizes living in harmony with the Tao (or Dao). The term Tao means "way", "path", or the "principle".

The Void (Supreme Mystery)

Wuji – ultimate stillness, the beginning of creation.

Yang Qi - yang refers to aspects or manifestations of Qi that are relatively positive: Also - immaterial, amorphous, expanding, hollow, light, ascending, hot, dry, warming, bright, aggressive, masculine and active.

Yin Qi - yin refers to aspects or manifestations of Qi that are relatively negative: Also - material, substantial, condensing, solid, heavy, descending, cold, moist, cooling, dark, female, passive and quiescent.

Taijitu - The term taijitu in modern Chinese is commonly used to mean the simple "divided circle" form (), but it may refer to any of several schematic diagrams that contain at least one circle with an inner pattern of symmetry representing yin and yang.

Yi – intellect, manifests as spirit-infused intelligence and understanding.

Baihui point - Governing Vessel 20 (GV 20). Sits on the crown of the head.

Jade Pillow – located at the top of the cervical vertebrae (C1).

Great Hammer – located on the midline at the base of the neck, between seventh cervical vertebra and first thoracic vertebra.

Mingmen point – Conception Vessel 6 (CV6), the 'Sea of Qi' located on the lower abdomen.

Qihai point – Conception Vessel 6 (CV6), the 'Sea of Qi' located on the lower abdomen.

Hui Yin point – Conception Vessel 1 (CV1), also known as the base chakra, is located between the genitals and the anus; the part of the body called the perineum.

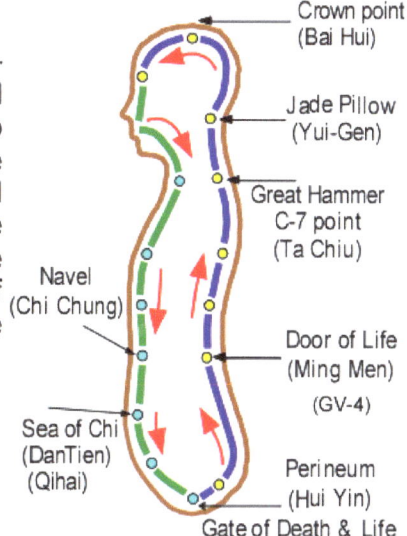

Wu Xing or 5 Elements -
The 5 Element theory is a major component of thought within Traditional Chinese Medicine (TCM). Each element represents natural aspects within our world. Natural cycles and interrelationships between these elements, is the basis for this theory. These elements have corresponding relationships within our environment as well as within our own being.

Zang-Fu organs – solid, yin organs are Zang – yang and hollow organs are Fu.

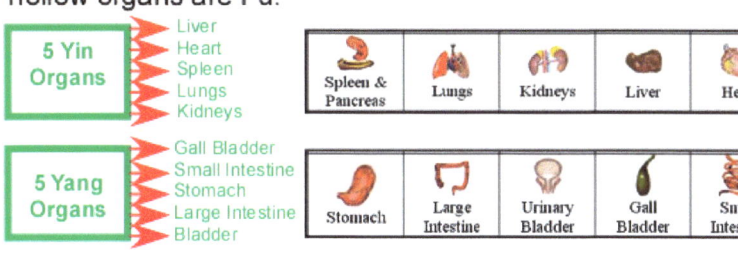

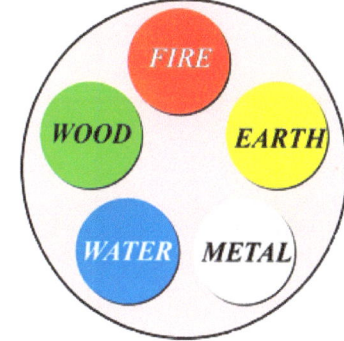

About the Instructor, Author & Artist - Jim Moltzan

My fitness training started at the age of 16 and has continued for almost 45 years. During that time, I attended high school, then college, and worked 2 jobs all while pursuing further training in martial arts and other fitness methods. Many years ago, I started up an additional business to help finance my next goal of owning my own school. I moved to Florida from the Midwest to make this goal a reality. Having owned two wellness and martial arts schools, I have surpassed what I once believed to be my potential. At this stage in my life, I have chosen not to open any more schools, as I found the business aspects took too much focus away from my true passion: training and teaching others.

Beyond my professional endeavors, I am also a husband and father of two grown children. I believe that we must be prepared to work hard mentally, physically and financially to earn our good health and well-being. Not only for ourselves but for our families as well. Good health always comes at a cost whether in time, effort, cost, sacrifice or some combination of the previous.

I returned to college in my later 50's, to pursue my BS in Holistic Health (wellness and alternative medicine). My degree program covered many wide-ranging topics such as anatomy and physiology, meditation, massage, nutrition, herbology, chemistry, biology, history and basis of various medical modalities such as allopathic, Traditional Chinese Medicine, Ayurveda/yoga, naturopathy, chiropractic, and complimentary alternative methods. I also studied religion, mythology of the world, stress relief/management as well as sociology, psychology (human behavior) and cultural issues associated with better health and wellness.

Most of the movements I teach and write about originate from Chinese martial arts. The Qigong (breathing work) is from Chinese Kung Fu and the Korean Dong Han medical Qigong lineage. I have also gained much knowledge of Traditional Chinese Medicine (TCM) from many TCM practitioners, martial arts masters, teachers and peers. This includes many techniques and practices of acupressure (reflexology, auricular, Jing Well, etc.), acupuncture, moxibustion as well as preparation of some herbal remedies and extracts for conditioning and injuries. I have been studying for over 20 years with Zen Wellness, learning medical Qigong as well as other Eastern methods of fitness, philosophy and self-cultivation. I have been recognized as a "Gold Coin" master instructor having trained and taught others for at least 10000 hours or roughly over 35 years. The core fitness movements are from Kung Fu and its forms in Tai Chi, Baguazhang, Dao Yin and Ship Pal Gi (Korean Kung Fu and weapons training). Each martial art has mental, physical and spiritual aspects that can complement and enhance one another. The more ways that you can move your body and engage your mind, the better it is for your overall health.

Physical health, mental well-being and the relationships within our lives; are these the most cherished aspects of our existence? Yet, how much effort do we put towards improving these areas on a daily basis?

Many have used martial arts and other mind-body methods of training as methods of learning to see one's character as others see them. I feel that I can offer the priceless qualities of truth, honor and integrity with my instruction. You must seek the right teacher for you, because in time a student can become similar to their teacher. Through the training that I have experienced and offer to others, an individual can understand and hopefully reach their full potential.

By developing self-discipline to continuously execute and perfect sets of movements, an individual can start to understand not only how they work physically but also mentally and emotionally. You can find your strengths and your weaknesses and improve them both. Through disciplined training, one not only enhances physical abilities but also cultivates mental resilience, allowing them to achieve their fullest potential in all areas of life.

I have co-authored a book, produced numerous other books and journals, graphic charts and study guides related to the mind and body connection and how it relates to martial arts, fitness, and self-improvement. A few hundred of my classes and lectures are viewable on YouTube.com.

Lineage

- Recognized as a 1000 and 10,000-hour student and teacher
- Earned gold coins through the Doh Yi Masters and Zen Wellness program
- Earned a 5th degree in Korean Kung Fu through the Dong Han lineage

Education

Bachelor of Science in Holistic Medicine - Vermont State University

Books Available Through Amazon

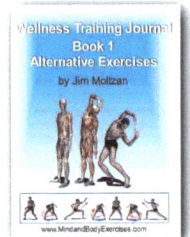   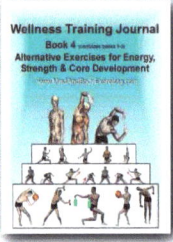  

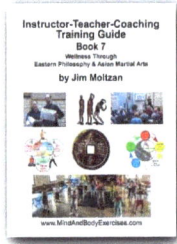  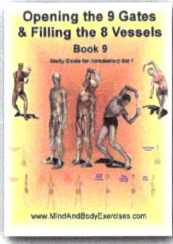 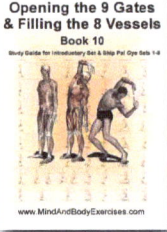 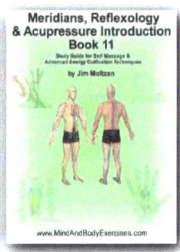 

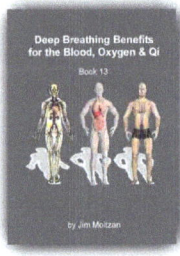 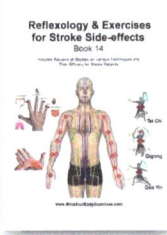 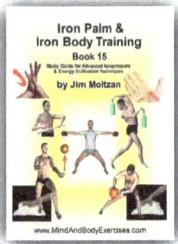 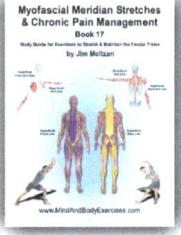 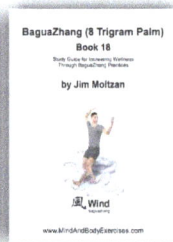 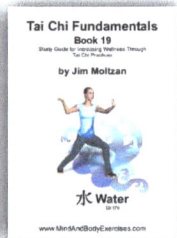

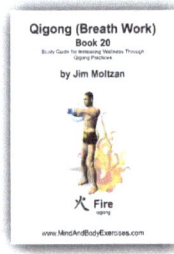 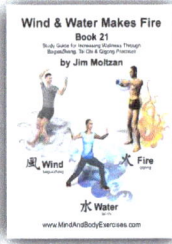 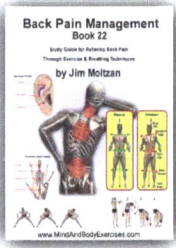  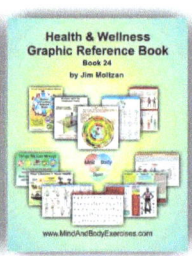 

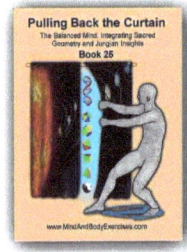 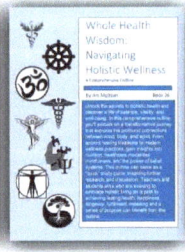 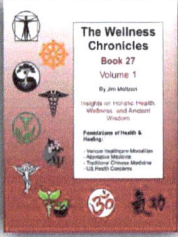  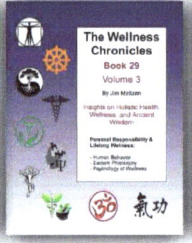 

Book Titles by Jim Moltzan

Book 1 - Alternative Exercises

Book 2 - Core Training

Book 3 - Strength Training

Book 4 - Combo of 1-3

Book 5 - Energizing Your Inner Strength

Book 6 - Methods to Achieve Better Wellness

Book 7 - Coaching & Instructor Training Guide

Book 8 - The 5 Elements & the Cycles of Change

Book 9 - Opening the 9 Gates & Filling 8 Vessels-Intro Set 1

Book 10 - Opening the 9 Gates & Filling 8 Vessels-sets 1 to 8

Book 11 - Meridians, Reflexology & Acupressure

Book 12 - Herbal Extracts, Dit Da Jow & Iron Palm Liniments

Book 13 - Deep Breathing Benefits for the Blood, Oxygen & Qi

Book 14 - Reflexology for Stroke Side Effects:

Book 15 - Iron Body & Iron Palm

Book 17 - Fascial Train Stretches & Chronic Pain Management

Book 18 - BaguaZhang

Book 19 - Tai Chi Fundamentals

Book 20 - Qigong (breath-work)

Book 21 - Wind & Water Make Fire

Book 22 - Back Pain Management

Book 23 - Journey Around the Sun-2nd Edition

Book 24 - Graphic Reference Book

Book 25 - Pulling Back the Curtain

Book 26 - Whole Health Wisdom: Navigating Holistic Wellness

Book 27 - The Wellness Chronicles (volume 1)

Book 28 - The Wellness Chronicles (volume 2)

Book 29 - The Wellness Chronicles (volume 3)

Book 30 - The Wellness Chronicles (complete edition, volumes 1-3)

Book 31 - Warrior, Scholar, Sage

Book 32 - The Wellness Chronicles (volume 4)

Book 33 - The Wellness Chronicles (volume 5)

Book 34 - Blindfolded Discipline

Book 35 - The Path of Integrity

Other Products

Laminated Charts 8.5" x 11" or 11" x 17" - over 200 various graphics (check the website)

Qigong - Chi Kung
SKU: ChiKung

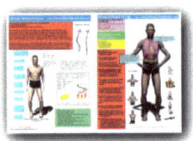

The human body is made up of bones, muscles, and organs amongst other components. Veins, arteries and capillaries carry blood and nutrients throughout to all of the systems and components. Additionally, 12 major energy medians carry the body's energy, "life force" also known as "chi". Ones chi is stored in the lower Dan Tien. Daily emotional imbalances accumulate tension and stress gradually affecting all of the body's systems. Each discomfort, nuisance, irritation or grudge continues to tighten and squeeze the flow of the life force. This is where "dis-ease" claims its foothold.

Strengthen Your Back (set #1)
SKU: StrengthenYourBack1

Good health of the lower back starts with good posture. The following set of exercises develop strength and flexibility which improve posture. Strength in the back, hips and abdominals provide a strong cage that houses the internal organs. Flexibility in these areas helps to maintain good blood circulation to the organs and lower body. Lengthening of the spine while exercising reduces stress and tension on the nervous system.

Broadsword 1-10
SKU: Broadsword

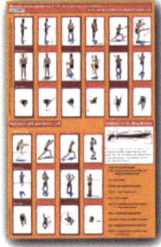

Broadsword training develops the body, mind and spirit well beyond that which can gained from empty hand training alone. The Broadsword has many different sets to be mastered utilizing quick, fluid and precise movements.

Ship Pal Gye set 7 (Kung Fu stance training)
SKU: ShipPalGye7

SHIP PAL GYE or Ship Par Gay, is a Korean version of Chinese Shaolin Lohan Qigong, meaning "18 chi movements" or what were supposedly the original 18 drills that Bodhidharma introduced to the Shaolin monks. It is reputed to be the basis for the Shaolin Kung Fu, which in turn, greatly influenced the developments of all branches of Asian fighting arts.

Noble Stances
SKU: NobleStances

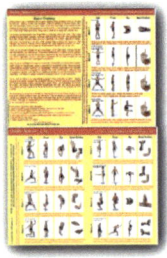

Noble stances are a combination of various stances from different styles of Chinese martial arts. Stances, in this case, meaning correct placement of the feet, knees, hips, and arm positions relative to ones center of gravity. Executing static positions and holding the particular body positions for anyway from a few seconds to several minutes reaps many benefits foremost being able to cultivate a strong and healthy core.

CONTACTS

For more information regarding charts, products, classes and instruction:

www.MindAndBodyExercises.com
info@MindAndBodyExercises.com

www.youtube.com/c/MindandBodyExercises
www.MindAndBodyExercises.wordpress.com

407-234-0119

Social Media:

Facebook:	MindAndBodyExercises
Instagram:	MindAndBodyExercises
Twitter:	MindAndBodyExercise

Jim Moltzan - Mind and Body Exercises
522 Hunt Club Blvd. #305
Apopka, FL 32703

Website

Blog

YouTube Channel